The Mecca Diaries

RAYDA JACOBS

DOUBLE
STOREY
a juta company

First published in 2005 by
Double Storey Books,
a division of Juta & Co. Ltd, Mercury Crescent,
Wetton, Cape Town

© 2005 Rayda Jacobs (text and photos)

ISBN 1 77013 018 7

All rights reserved. No part of this book may be reproduced or utilised in any form and by any means, electronic or mechanical, including photocopying and recording, or by any information storage or retrieval system, without permission in writing from the publisher.

Editing by *Helen Laurenso*n
Text design and layout by *Abdul Amien*
Cover design by *Abdul Amien*
Cover photograph of the author by *Karina Turok*
Printing by Paarl Print, Paarl

Contents

Acknowledgements *7*

The intention *9*

Preparation *12*

Leaving *19*

Arriving in Jeddah *25*

Medina the Radiant *32*

Inside Mecca *52*

Hajj *114*

Do's and don'ts for hajj *155*

Glossary *159*

Acknowledgements

Always Mecca has been a mystery to me: a place of the prophets, somewhere in the desert in the centre of the earth. My interest might have started with my grandmother, 45 years ago. I was a child, and remember the excitement around her impending trip. She had sold ice blocks with condensed milk to save up her pennies, and for months I had had to go over her lessons with her. But I was apprehensive about this place she would go to, and remember her coming home after what seemed like an eternity. She was dressed in cream, with a black cloak and a cream *medorah* threaded with gold. There were lots of people coming to see her; the atmosphere was festive, with cakes and cooldrinks, and the dates and mebos she'd brought from Mecca.

Later, on my own journey, when I thought of her in her fancy shoes with her feet that were always hurting, I couldn't imagine what hajj must've been like for her. In those days you would leave on a boat and be away for six months. You would take crates of food along. There were no airconditioned buses and no tents at Mina, Arafah and Muzdalifah, where the toilets were constructed out of three pieces of zinc and had a lappie at the entrance. When a hajji came back, the stories took you way into the night.

I am grateful for the teachings of this grandmother, who never failed to remind me of God.

A special word of thanks to my friend Arnulf Kolstad, who provided me with a digital camera, and to my publishers, Bridget Impey and Russell Martin, for taking me out to lunch two weeks before my trip and talking me into writing a book.

Rayda Jacobs
April 2005

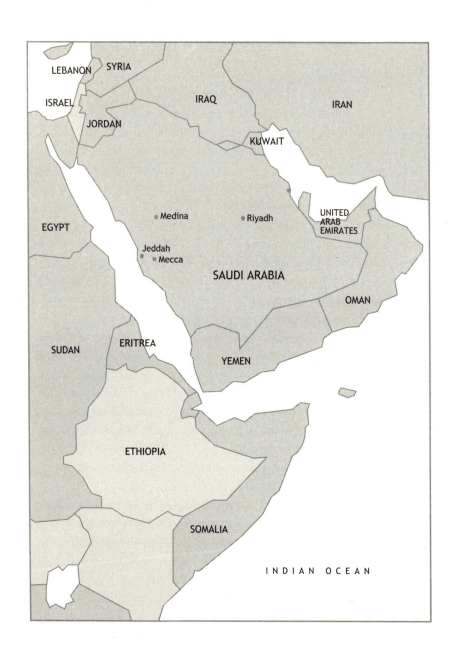

Early Mecca

The intention

 remember the first time I expressed a desire to go to Mecca. I was living in Toronto. I was at my sister's house, enjoying Thanksgiving dinner with friends. I talked about going on hajj over stuffed turkey and cranberry sauce, having good intentions, but not really being in a position of readiness. I was attracted to the notion of going, to the experience I might have. I really had no clue what it entailed.

Going on hajj starts with the *niyyah:* the intention to go. Once you have made this *niyyah,* you also perform special *istigarah* prayers and ask God if this is the right time for you to perform hajj. Hajj is a serious contemplation. It's not a holiday; it's not a trip you decide to take at the last minute. Years of self-communion have brought you to this point. Hajj is about absolution: you are going to Mecca to seek God's forgiveness. The pilgrim makes his or her way to the centre in the same way that man makes his pilgrimage towards God. The word 'hajj' literally means to travel. It also means effort – exertion in the path of God – to dominate the self. Hajj is the fifth of the religious duties of a Muslim. Every adult is compelled to go once during his or her lifetime to Mecca, if able, in order to perform there the great effort of training the self to comply with the commands of Allah and to submit willingly to His Will.

And so, almost two decades later, I made my *niyyah* to go. You can make a *niyyah* even with no money. The main thing is that your intention must be right. But I had other concerns. When I looked at the people around me who were going on hajj, they appeared to be on solid ground: they were dressed properly, they could recite *ayahs* (Qur'anic verses) from memory. In all likelihood, they performed their prayers on time, and gave to the poor. To go to Mecca you have to have your spiritual ducks in a row. Was I worthy of such a trip?

I told my friend, Judy, of my desire to go. She asked how much the trip would cost. I said about R40 000. She opened her purse and gave me R200 to start a hajj fund. For a month, no other monies went into the account, and then boom! – a week later, *Confessions of a Gambler* won the Herman Charles Bosman Prize and fetched R20 000. The following week, it nabbed the *Sunday Times* Fiction Award, also for R50 000. This was surely the hand of God. I had received my invitation.

I was ready to go. But the next hurdle was, with whom would I go? I couldn't go to Mecca on my own: I was an unmarried woman. A woman can undertake hajj only with a husband or a family member she cannot marry. If it is her first hajj, however, she cannot be denied entry, and can have someone act as her *mahram*. The *mahram* is responsible for her during the trip. If anything should happen to her, or if she should die during her stay in Mecca, he will have the authority to deal with the Saudis.

Around the same time as I was contemplating all of this in June 2004, a friend of my sister came to visit, and told me that she and her husband were going to Mecca in December with some members of her husband's family. They were going with the Royal International Group. Pilgrims can enter Mecca during hajj only with a group, whose leaders have to take care of all the paperwork with the Saudis, book the accommodation and oversee everything related to the pilgrims' movements while on hajj. A group will have several spiritual leaders to look after the *hujaj*.

I listened to her talk and wondered if it had been God's will that she had come to visit me that day. I told her that I wanted to go to Mecca also, but that I didn't have anyone to go with, and didn't have a *mahram* as no male relative in my family was going on hajj that year.

'Come with us,' she said.

'Are you sure? You haven't even asked your husband.'

'He will say it's okay.'

'What about my *mahram*?'

'We'll sort it out. We'll ask the Imam. Hajj classes are starting next week. The others are going to classes in town, it's closer for them. We're going to Imam Pandy.'

Preparation

On a cool night in July, I put on my robe and scarf and drove to the house of the woman I was to go with, just around the corner from me. We would go together to hajj classes in her husband's car. Going to classes was the beginning. It meant we were serious. We had no idea what we would hear, but were eager for the experience.

Imam Pandy held his classes at home, in a huge garage provided with trestle tables and glasses of water. Men sat in the first three rows and the women in the last two. There were more than 50 people in robes and scarves and fezzes present. In front, where the Imam stood, were a microphone and a table with books. On the wall were large glossy pictures of the holy sites in Mecca and Medina. Imam Pandy, a man of slight build in his fifties, with lively eyes and an impish look, stood waiting. When everyone was seated, he said an opening prayer and the class was under way.

The friend and I sat at the back. Her husband sat with the men. We had each bought a book on hajj before taking our seats.

I watched Imam Pandy talk about the requirements for hajj. I had known him as a child. His mother and my mother had been friends, and I had gone to their shop and played with his sisters. As I grew up and stopped going out with my mother, I didn't see the Pandys again. In those days I had called him by his first name. Now I called him Imam.

Imam Pandy was with the Al Anwar Group, a group known for their efficiency and for looking after their *hujaj*. We were attending his classes on Wednesday nights, but would be travelling with the Royal International Group. We were going with Royal because we had connections with them, and a special package had been procured for the six of us. Imams don't mind whose classes you attend and there are no fees involved. Most people who attend a particular spiritual leader's class ultimately go with his group. However, if it doesn't happen that way, it doesn't matter.

We opened our books on the first page. We were astounded by the amount of information contained in them: the contents list had 61 headings. There were the *shuroots* (conditions) of hajj, the ways in which hajj could be performed, a prayer for leaving the house, a prayer for the vehicle, a prayer when starting a journey to the holy city, a prayer at the *kab'r* of the holy Prophet Muhammad, a prayer when donning the *ihram*, what to do, where to do it, how to behave. The book covered every aspect of hajj. Memorisation of the long prayers in Arabic was perhaps the most daunting.

'You don't have to remember everything,' Imam Pandy said. 'You will have your books, and your leaders will be there. And you don't have to agonise about memorising the Arabic. You can speak in whatever language you want. God understands all languages.'

Later, listening to Imam Alexander's tapes on hajj, I heard him make the same point. 'I speak to God in Afrikaans,' he says. 'As long as you are saying what you are supposed to say. This is not an Arabic God, or an English God. God understands all languages.'

At a dinner months later for the *hujaj*, we were told: 'One of the most important requirements for hajj is *sab'r*. You will need a lot of patience. From the moment you arrive in Jeddah you will be tested. You might have to wait four or six hours for a bus to take you into Medina. And then the bus arrives, and the driver first has to have his tea, and then his cigarette. And when he is ready, you leave.

'Here, when you are travelling, you are travelling by South African rules. There, you are travelling by their rules. Don't try to be smart with the Arab. And please, I will repeat this: a woman must not walk up to Immigration in Jeddah by herself. That single act alone can hold up a bus for six hours. She must walk up to Immigration with her *mahram*. The *mahram* must speak for her.

'And keep your suitcase key on your person. When you arrive, don't wait for the Arab to tell you to open your case. Make it easy for him. Open your bags, and tell him to *bismillah*, and look through your things. And keep a black pen on you, and a copy of your passport. You will have to fill out a lot of forms. And have your own pen. Don't hold up the group by waiting for someone else's pen.

'Remember, people, Mecca is crowded. You will be jostled on all sides, especially during the last days of hajj when Mecca is full. You can't lose your cool. If you are in *ihram*, and someone accidentally knocks into you during *tawaaf* and you give him a dirty look or grumble, you have violated your hajj and must pay a *dumm*. A *dumm* is the equivalent of one sheep, usually R700. The sheep are slaughtered and given to the poor. All pilgrims will automatically include the cost of at least one *dumm* in their expenses. If you don't follow the rules of hajj, you will pay many *dumms*.'

Imam Pandy talked. I looked at the page devoted to the medical advice. Compulsory immunisation included yellow fever and meningitis. We were also advised to take flu shots, and to carry on with our present medication. Health hazards included sunstroke and heatstroke, and we were not to drink excessive quantities of iced drinks, but rather bottled mineral water and *zamzam*. *Zamzam* is water from the spring which had first gushed forth when Hagar went in search of water for her infant son, Ishmail. It was also recommended that we take along energy tablets, antibiotics, analgesics, anti-allergic cream, anti-emetic tablets for nausea, laxatives, plasters, etc. Salt tablets to prevent dehydration are also sometimes advised, although it is probably better to take an electrolyte solution that contains salt, such as Energade or Game in powdered or concentrate form.

'And please, people, when you go down to the Haram, make sure you've taken your medication and have what you need with you. Don't get down there and then send somebody back to your room for your teeth. Moenie vergeet om julle tande in te sit nie.'

For a tiny guy, he had a great sense of humour, and we were to enjoy it many times over the next few months in his classes. He was full of pep, full of anecdotes. But with the laughter and camaraderie, also came the seriousness of hajj. Hajj wasn't going off on a jaunt to some holiday spot. There were preparations and obligations that had to be seen to before you could leave. You had to put your house in order. You couldn't have debt. Car payments and bond payments had to be taken care of. In the case of a bond, you had to appoint a temporary executor in the event of your death. You needed a will that made provision for the fact that you were travelling. You had to leave enough money to take care of the people at home while you were away.

'Don't go to Mecca and leave your family at home unable to pay the phone bill. If you don't have enough money, perhaps you are not ready to go. There's next year, or the year after. And make sure you have enough money on you for the duration of your trip. Don't get there and run out of money and be a burden to someone else.'

Greeting is another tradition particular to the Cape. A prospective pilgrim goes in person to visit family and friends, and asks for their blessings and good wishes and prayers. Usually a specific friend has the honour of driving you around to your friends, and greeting might take several weekends.

'You go first to your family, and then to your friends. And you go also to your neighbours, even if they are not Muslim neighbours. You don't know if you will see any of these people again.'

Greeting is more of a cultural ritual than a matter of informing people that you are leaving, because more often than not, people will already have heard that you are going to Mecca; but still you go to greet them. The more traditional, older *hujaj* like to greet in Afrikaans. Their greeting has rhythm and poignancy, and can be quite emotional.

'Salaam aleikoem. As Allah vir my vergun, gaan ek mushafee na die buit-ul-lah…'

You inform the person of the date you are leaving, and ask for a *duah*, that God might grant you good health, and safe passage to and from Mecca, and that your hajj might be accepted.

Because greeting can take time, and because people live far apart and are sometimes not in when you call, the Imam recommends the month of Ramadan as people are bound to be home then. If they're out, you leave a card with the same greeting, giving details of departure. Cards differ in style. Some might list all the places in Mecca to which you are travelling. Others, like my own card, are very simple.

Another aspect of greeting is the pardon you must seek for anything you might have said or done in the past to the person you are greeting.

'Don't wait for the last minute to ask forgiveness,' Imam Pandy advises. 'You have this brother you had a fall-out with years ago, and now you wait until a few days before you leave, and he's forced to forgive you, because if he doesn't he'll feel guilty that your hajj might not be accepted. And so he forgives you, and you come back, and you still have it in for one another. Go make your peace now, and work through your problems.'

It was an informative evening. I could see the benefits of attending hajj classes. Hajj classes take you through the experience. You end up knowing everything, from etiquette to what to take with you to what to do if you should suddenly find yourself lost in a crowd of a million strangers.

'Don't panic. In Medina, for instance, there's a fountain in front of the Prophet's Mosque. Familiarise yourself with this fountain when you come out of your hotel. If you should get lost, ask anyone where the fountain is. There's only one fountain in Medina. When you get to the fountain, you'll see your hotel.'

The South African pilgrim is said to be the most informed and best-behaved of all pilgrims – all due to the preparation done beforehand.

The class ends. We go up to the Imam to discuss the question of who might be my *mahram*.

'You can be her *mahram*,' he says immediately, referring to my friend's husband.

And that was that. I had a group, I had a *mahram*; I could make my plans. We thanked the Imam and promised to be back the following week.

Out on the street, the husband said to me, 'Who would've thought I would end up being your *mahram*?'

'What do you mean?' I asked.

'At your 21st birthday party, you accused me of stealing your LP.'

'What? Are you serious?'

'Yes. You said I had stood next to the hi-fi, and had taken it.'

'Oh, my word, I don't remember.'

'You did. I remember it clearly.'

I was laughing now. 'Well, if you say I did it, it must be true. That was a wicked and a silly girl back then. But you kept it in all these years?'

'Yes. But I never forgot.'

'Well, then, let me sommer ask you right now for your forgiveness. Do you forgive me?'

He laughed. 'Of course.'

After a few months, the hajj classes came to an end. We knew we would never remember everything we had learned, but had a good understanding of what we were about to embark on. We also had our books and our spiritual leaders who would take us through all the steps once we were there.

Two weeks before Ramadan, shortly after sunrise one Sunday morning, we met with hundreds of other *hujaj* at the shrine of Sheikh Yusuf in Faure. Sheikh Yusuf was from Indonesia, and had been exiled by the Dutch to the Cape of Good Hope in the late 1600s, with a group of 49 followers. He was isolated at Macassar, some distance from Cape

Town, where it was hoped he would not have much contact with other slaves. Our visit to the kramat was not for purposes of worship, but rather a sign of respect to the political exiles, slaves and royalty who had brought Islam to our shores.

We made a short *duah*, and continued on to two other kramats at Camps Bay and Constantia. Visiting the kramats is a tradition, not a prerequisite for hajj. And there are Muslims who don't visit the kramats at all. But it's a nice way to spend a morning, and creates a great feeling of community to see so many *hujaj* with their families and their picnic baskets and good cheer. A face you see in another group might be the one you recognise in a crowded Mecca street when you are lost.

Leaving

A week before departure, it is open house at the pilgrim's home. You can expect people at any time during the day, and until late at night. There are trestle tables with bowls of sweets and nuts and dried fruit and cakes, and pies and samoosas, and other nibbles that visitors might bring along. People sit with you, tell their own stories of Mecca and give tips and advice; and when they leave, they usually slip you an envelope with money in it, known as a *slavat*.

Eight days before my departure, an old friend, Gadidja, came to visit me on a Sunday morning. I had just finished baking a banana and date cake, and offered her some. She talked about her own experiences in the holy land, offered some tips, and then opened her purse; she said she hadn't used all her money in Mecca and handed me 50 rials. I was touched. It was money that had come from Mecca, and was going back with me to Mecca.

'At least when you get to Jeddah,' she said, 'you don't have to worry about changing your money right away. You have enough here for food for a few days.'

Gadidja left, and another friend, Karnita, arrived with her husband, Abas. Karnita had called the day before to make sure I would be home, and wanted to visit when my house wouldn't be so full of people, and she would be able to talk. She came with a gift: she had bought me a pair of white socks, and wanted me to wear them when I performed my first *umrah* – circumambulation around the Kab'ah, seven times.

She also brought me unscented soap – a requirement for a particular part of the hajj – and a special hand towel and facecloth, for when I got into *ihram* the first time. The *ihram* for a woman is a white robe, white scarf, white petticoat and long white pants. For a man, it is two pieces of unstitched white cloth: one wrapped around the waist, and one worn over the naked shoulder.

I accepted the gifts graciously, and said that while I would wear the socks for my first *umrah*, I had already received the towels and facecloth from my cousin, Adela, and would have to use Adela's towels when I prepared to don my *ihram*. She was happy for me just to use them.

The same Sunday, around ten at night, I was in bed when the phone rang. My son answered and called me to the phone. It was a woman who asked if I remembered Blinde Tietie. I knew two people who were referred to as Blinde Tietie, and just said yes. She said that I didn't know her now, but that she had known me as a little girl, and was related to me in some way. She had just come from some people and she had heard there that I was going to Mecca, and was calling to tell me that she was very proud of me, that she wished me well, and that she was coming to see me in the week.

The thing about going on hajj is that whoever knows you and hears the news comes to the house. There is no need for an invitation. You might greet ten people, and 200 show up at your house. The gratitude you feel is overwhelming. There is so much love, so much concern. You go on a holiday, and none of this happens. But this is Mecca. You are undertaking a spiritual journey: everyone wants to be part of it. Another friend wanted to give me her *ihram* to wear, and was clearly disappointed when I told her that I had already bought two sets of everything. Everyone wants some item of clothing to travel to Mecca, and come back blessed.

As the time drew near, my house started to fill up. People came and went all day. My sister, Shiraz, came after her job at the office to take charge of the kitchen and the eats. One person fried samoosas, another served tea, one baked pies, yet another filled up the plates with cakes and sweets and greeted people as they came in. There was no place to move. Two days before departure, on a Sunday, we had the family lunch. Shiraz made beef breyani and chicken curry. There was mince curry also. By ten that evening, we were exhausted; and still the doorbell rang, and more people visited.

The woman who had called a few days earlier to say she was coming to see me made an appearance with her son and daughter-in-law and three children. It was interesting to hear stories about her early days with my mother. I didn't know that the two of them had worked together. And she had other stories too. Everyone listened and the conversation around the table was pleasant and animated. Some time before one in the morning, I dropped into bed, too tired to sleep.

The night before departure was hectic. Friends and family who had waited until the last minute now came to say their farewells. There was

no more room anywhere in the kitchen or in the garage to put any more of the cakes and biscuits they brought along. The tables groaned under platters of pies and samoosas and other eats. I saw cousins whom I hadn't seen in years; friends who'd heard from other friends; both my publishers; my friend, Judy, who'd given me the R200 to start my hajj fund. Another special friend, Amina, a *toekamandie* – a person who washes the dead – made a farewell *duah*. My suitcase was blessed, and all that was in it, and prayers were offered for my safe passage to Mecca, and safe return. By the time the visitors left and everything had been cleaned up, the day of departure had dawned.

Day 1 – Tuesday December 14th 2004

The morning of my departure was emotional. I had wondered how I would feel, and here it was. My sister arrived shortly after 6.00 a.m. to see to sandwiches and coffee for the guests. I had asked Sheikh Seraj Hendricks, from the Azzavia Mosque, to make the farewell *duah*. I was leaving my house for six weeks and I was leaving my son, Faramarz. I was also leaving Georgina, who'd come to work for me three years before, when I'd

needed someone to help me with my mother, who'd had a stroke and who had died earlier in the year that was now ending. I was leaving behind my Siberian husky, China, and my son's German shepherd, Tupac. I had had China straight from her mother when she was just six weeks old, ten years ago.

At 8.00 a.m. Sheikh Seraj Hendricks started to make *duah*. There were sniffles and sobs. As I listened to the words, it hit me that I really would get on a plane and go to the holy land. It was no longer words; it was reality. I was going to the place where Abraham had first walked in the desert and talked about the oneness of God,

and where the holy Prophet Muhammad (peace be upon him) had revived monotheism centuries later.

Was I deserving of such a gift?

My brother, Hymie, sobbed into my shoulder. My sister was red-eyed and emotional. The line stretched from the living room to the kitchen, out the door, and into the street, as everyone waved goodbye.

At the airport I met the other people I would be travelling with. We were on our way.

1.00 p.m. We arrive at Johannesburg airport. We have a seven-hour wait. The airport is swarming with travellers and *hujaj*. We can't check in our luggage or change currency without our passports. The spiritual leader is to meet us at 4.00 p.m. to hand us visas and passports. At 5.00 p.m. he is still not there. We're to board at 7.00 p.m. At ten to six, he arrives.

In the midst of all this, we are not to neglect our prayers. There are special prayer and ablution facilities on the third floor. There are six of us. We take turns going upstairs so there can always be someone to watch the luggage. I make it just in time to go to Customs to declare my laptop and camera so that I don't have a problem on my return.

At last it is time to book in our luggage. The airport is crowded. I am on my way to the line – a special queue for *hujaj* travelling on Egypt Air. I see one of the women in my group standing talking to someone. She waves for us to go on ahead to the line, but remains standing where she is. Her husband has her luggage and his own on a trolley; the others have their luggage on trolleys also: three trolleys moving slowly up the line. We are a few feet away from the counter, and we can't find her. She has the passports and tickets and her husband can't proceed without her. He goes to look for her, but to no avail. After some minutes, she appears. The incident is not a catastrophe, but is an indication of what can happen if we don't advise one another when we go off on our own. Johannesburg airport is crowded, but this is nothing like the hordes of people we're going to encounter in Medina and Mecca. It's a good reminder for us to be aware at all times of how easy it is to get lost.

We pass through immigration. A man from the SAHUC (South African Hujaj & Umrah Council) ensures that things move smoothly, and even makes arrangements with the pilot of the aircraft to allow the *hujaj* to board a few minutes late so that we may first perform the sunset prayers. In a quiet corner on the second floor of the terminal building, the men take up their positions in front, and the women stand behind them in rows. We perform our prayers. We board.

By the time we are in our seats, we are tired. At the same time, we're excited. After an eight-hour journey, we arrive in Cairo at about three in the morning. The airport is deserted. A handful of officials look at our passports, and we sit in a room with our bags waiting for 7.00 a.m. Finally we board the next flight.

Day 2 – Wednesday December 15th 2004

We arrive at the Hajj Terminal in Jeddah at around ten in the morning. This is not the international airport, but an airport that operates only once during the year, for a few weeks during hajj, and then is closed again. It is huge enough to accommodate the three million pilgrims who all have to pass through on their way to Medina and Mecca, and then home again, in a very short space of time.

We enter the airport building and meet in a large room with long rows of benches. Up ahead is a wire fence with a gate, attended by several young Saudi clerks in brown uniforms and berets. There are also some officials in white robes and red scarves, in glass-enclosed cubicles, checking passports – two or three clerks per cubicle. We wait almost an hour before our documents have been inspected and re-inspected and double-checked, before being handed back to us. By this

time my passport has taken on the look of a coupon book, with my yellow vaccination certificate stapled inside, a Saudi visa and barcodes in several colours.

I am allowed through and have to hand the passport to another stern-looking official at the door, after which I receive a dismissive wave of the hand, as if to say, Go woman, that way. After picking up our luggage we go outside, to a bank of white-robed and red-scarved officials sitting at a long table, asking for our passports again. We pay our *tanazul* of US $275: a fee for the different services the Saudi government provides for pilgrims during hajj. And we are happy to pay. To cater for three million pilgrims during hajj is no joke. To organise the sanitation at Mina, Muzdalifah and Arafah, as well as the water trucks, the hospital services, the cleaning of the Haram – to manage the monstrous task of directing traffic and keeping control of hordes of people all there for the same purpose, at the same time – it all takes a lot of doing.

Outside, we see Tent City – the huge tents vaulted overhead, stretching out into the distance. This is where pilgrims from different countries will all be allocated a spot to wait with their luggage, either for a bus to take them into Medina or Mecca, or on the homebound journey, to wait for a plane.

Our bags are loaded onto a motorised baggage carrier, and we walk behind it for a good few minutes to an empty location with benches. The bags are offloaded, and we're told that we'll wait a few hours for a bus. We've been warned beforehand that there will be a lot of waiting around.

We look around us. Tent City is airy and filled with pilgrims from different parts of the world. A hundred feet away stands a row of brightly-coloured, airconditioned busses. These are for the pilgrims already in *ihram* who are going direct to Mecca. We're going to Jeddah; we have to wait. But we don't mind a few hours of stretching our legs after so many hours in

the air. We need to freshen up and take ablution for prayers. We'll have our first squat on the dreaded toilet. I had heard about this kind of toilet, and had built up all kinds of images in my head. On this particular afternoon, however, I am

pleasantly surprised. I open the door, and there it is: a brown porcelain hole in the floor, which flushes like a regular toilet. A thin little hose coming out of the wall gives you a quick spray between the legs. We have had so many tips from friends on how to overcome the indignities of the squatting toilet that we have each come prepared with a piece of elastic which we pull on over our clothes, then haul up with our robes so that when we crouch down, our hems don't drag on the wet floor. I am grateful for that tip. Perching in this undignified position, wearing a robe and a long scarf – holding everything up – using the spray, locating the tissue – is quite a manoeuvre.

3.00 p.m. We are finally told that a bus is waiting for us. Two young Saudis in crisp white robes and red scarves, speaking intermittently into walkie-talkies, tell us to stand in two rows: one for the women and one for the men. We have to walk single file, like schoolchildren, to the bus. We board. The luggage is loaded on. The driver gets in. Everyone is counted and re-counted. I look out the window as the bus pulls away. Young Arab men are standing around in groups talking, or strolling about.

'Don't they have any work to do?' someone asks. 'And look at their feet. Hulle voete is almal te groot vir hulle sandals.'

She was right. Most of them had their heels hanging over the edges. But they are handsome young men. I sense a restlessness in them. They seem to have nothing to do.

In the bus, the airconditioning is directly overhead, and shoots a cold stream of air at my shoulder. Everywhere people are fiddling with

the controls, covering themselves with jerseys and towels. The bus driver nods at our requests for him to turn down the airconditioning, but does nothing. In the end, I sit with my prayer mat draped over my back.

Outside the window, the land is yellow and brown, rocky and barren. After some hours, it changes to black and grey stone. The bus drones on. We pass by derelict little buildings with no windows and no doors, the odd little shop, an occasional petrol station with no customers – reminding me of a strip on the edge of a ghost town. The sun starts to go down. As the bus drifts down the highway, its passengers fast asleep, it seems as if we're floating in space: no music, no talking, just gentle breathing, and rows of slumped bodies as we give in to fatigue.

The bus stops for 40 minutes at a restaurant where we can have something to drink and eat and freshen up. It's prayer time. We have to take ablution. This is a remote, backwoods kind of place, except that there are no backwoods: it's situated along the highway travelling through the desert to Medina. There's a humble, dusty little building with sacks of rice and other foodstuffs, with SUPER MARKET painted in big letters on the whitewashed wall. A mosque stands waiting in the

process of being renovated, the ground surrounding it cluttered with cement dust and bricks and planks, and there's a dark-looking restaurant with pilgrims filtering inside to where a group of men are sharing a platter of chicken and rice on the floor.

This is a family restaurant, so women are allowed in also. Still, I am careful not to be brazen, and ask one of the men in my party to go up to the counter with me. The man serving is tall, in his early forties, with a kind of cloth hat on his head, and a long brown cloth jacket over a robe. I ask if I can have a piece of chicken, without rice. He makes a sound with his teeth, which means yes. I ask if I can have it grilled. He says, 'Flame, flame.' I take this to mean that it will be grilled, and agree. He writes something on a piece of paper, and tells me to go to the end of the wall, to the fourth window. Then, without blinking an eye, he lifts up his leg and puts his foot, shoe and all, on top of the waist-high counter, and turns to the next customer. I look around to see if anyone is watching. But it seems to be nothing unusual. The man is just being his normal self. He is changing position, resting his foot on the food counter – and doesn't look one bit perturbed or uncomfortable in this strange position.

'What do you think?' I turn to my friend.

'Die's die Arab se land,' he says.

We get the chicken, but no one feels much like eating.

Back in the bus, we huddle under our jackets and prayer mats, shivering. We're nearing Medina. Sheikh Gabriels, who happens to be with us, for he too is going to perform hajj, gets up in the front of the bus and gives a short history of the holy Prophet Muhammad (pbuh), and his migration to the Radiant City.

We recite verses honouring the Prophet (pbuh) all the way into Medina and arrive at 10.30 at night. We're not at our destination yet, however. With pilgrims there's lots of red tape and paperwork, and first, we have to go to the Control Centre, where arriving and departing *hujaj* have to check in. We remain seated. Our passports are collected by our group leader and taken away. We wait almost an hour and a half before we get going again. Shortly before midnight, we check in at the al-Shourfah Hotel. It's one of the nicer hotels, and we have a suite with two bedrooms and a bathroom. Our bedroom is fair, with four beds and a large window. The two men in the party are in the room next to ours. We unpack, have a shower and drop into bed. We haven't slept in almost two days.

Three hours later, we hear the call to prayer. It is 5.30 a.m. We have overslept. We jump out of bed, take ablution, and head for the mosque for our first of 40 sets of prayers. It's our intention to catch 40 *waq'ts* – sets of prayers – in the mosque before we leave for Mecca. It's not compulsory or part of hajj – in fact, coming to Medina isn't part of the hajj, but it's part of the build-up, and it's hoped that if you come to the mosque for eight days in a row, not missing any of the five daily prayers, when you return to your own country you will continue to go to mosque, and be steadfast in your prayers.

The Prophet's Mosque

Medina the Radiant

Day 3 – Thursday December 16th 2004

To tell you about the moment I first saw the Prophet's Mosque is not something I can do easily. My expectations, years of reading and listening to stories of the life of the holy Prophet Muhammad (pbuh), and coming to the place where his earthly remains are buried – in the same spot where he died – came together in a moment that is too emotional to describe. I saw the minarets as I walked up from the hotel, but actually coming onto the *mataff* – the marble precinct surrounding the mosque where there is additional room for a million people to pray – I just stood there and cried. I was in the place. I was on the spot. Fourteen hundred years ago, there had been the Prophet's house (pbuh), and the houses of his wives. There had been the little mosque. I was in the place where Muhammad Mustafa had walked and prayed and talked with his Companions. I was in the place where he'd spent his last years and died. I was in the precinct of his last hours on earth. Perhaps my footsteps crossed his. Perhaps I was standing in the exact place where he'd alighted from his camel. I was in Medina al-Munawwarah, the City of the Prophet (pbuh). Writing this now, on a borrowed laptop, in my hotel room four minutes from the Haram, my eyes are filled with tears. How have I been so fortunate as to come here? As I stood on the *mataff*, I cried into my sleeve. *O God, I asked you to bring me here, and here I am – in front of the mosque and the final resting place of the holy Prophet Muhammad (pbuh).*

We were led by our group leader to one of the doors of the mosque, through which we would be able to see, from a distance, the *kab'r* of the Prophet (pbuh) and two of his most trusted Companions, the caliphs Um'r and Abu Bak'r. Only men could go in through that door, but women were allowed a glimpse a good distance back, behind a green wrought-iron fence. It was quite something to be standing there,

The kab'r of the Holy Prophet and two of his most trusted Companions, caliphs Um'r and Abu Bak'r

just a few hundred feet away from something I had longed to see. We had a sidelong view of the three gold doors behind which were the graves of the holy Prophet (pbuh) and his two Companions. I felt sorrowful that I wasn't allowed in to look up close, and asked one of the men later if he could see anything through the grille of the door.

'For less than a minute, and you're not allowed to get close. It's so full. The *asgharis* move you along. You can't stand there.'

'But what do you see? Can you see through the grille?'

'I saw, yes, it's all rural in there. It's the grave.'

The grave. I had a picture of what it might've looked like fourteen hundred years ago. They had buried the Prophet (pbuh) on the same spot where he'd died. His most trusted Companion, Abu Bak'r, had remembered the Prophet (pbuh) saying while he was alive that a prophet was always buried in the same spot where he died. He had died in the room of his favourite wife, Aisha, with his head in her lap. He had asked his other wives, when he knew he was gravely ill, if he could be with her for the last. It hadn't been Aisha's turn. They had agreed. And so they had buried him there. The house became a

mosque. The green dome was right over it. The entrance closest to the site was the entrance for males.

But women were allowed to come within proximity of the area inside the mosque. They were allowed four hours in the morning from 7.00 to 11.00, and again right after the midday prayers, for an hour or two. Men were allowed to go at any other time.

After a short prayer at the gate outside, the group leader told us that another woman in the group, Gadidja, would act as our leader and take us inside the mosque to Rawda-tul-Jannah – the Sacred Garden – where the Prophet (pbuh) is buried.

The mosque is an awesome structure to behold and stretches over several blocks. There are numerous entrances for both men and women: large, solid doors covered with brass. Since the Prophet's time (pbuh), the mosque has been extended several times, the last extension being completed as recently as 1994. The mosque has ten granite and gold-plated bronze minarets, 2 725 columns, 85 doors, 67 000 lighting fixtures and chandeliers, 543 cameras, and a praying capacity for up to 650 000. At times of hajj, *umrah* and Eid, the praying capacity stretches from the *mataff* into the streets and beyond.

And there's a reverence for entering the Prophet's Mosque that has to be observed. One has to have complete personal cleanliness, wear clean clothes, walk peacefully, not climb over the shoulders of others, not push seated persons, be quiet. A person with a bad smell is forbidden to enter the mosque, and it is recommended that one comes early to avoid arriving in a rush. Racing into the mosque displays bad manners and disrespect for such a holy place. Raising one's voice and idle talk are also unacceptable.

But before going into the mosque, we are shown the Baqi Cemetery a few hundred feet behind us, where the Prophet's wives (pbuh) and his Companions are buried. No entry is permitted, and there is nowhere for women to go to look over the fence. The only way a man might be able to take a look is if there's a funeral, and he slips in as one of the family. Pilgrims who die while in Medina are buried here also. The walls surrounding the cemetery have been raised as there are now some twenty more graves on top of the earlier ones – even on top of the graves of the Companions. Every prayer time, there are one or two *janazahs* – funerals – waiting.

Our tour on foot is over. At last it is time to go inside, to Rawda-tul-Jannah – the Sacred Garden – where the Prophet (pbuh) is interred. We follow Gadidja to a different entrance on the other side. We have our cloth bags over our shoulders with reading glasses, *kitaabs*, a Qur'an, tissues, a hand towel in the event we have to take ablution, and a separate cloth bag into which we put our shoes and carry them inside the mosque.

Female *asgharis* dressed in black cloaks and black head coverings, with only their eyes showing, search our bags. No cameras whatsoever, including cellphones able to take pictures, are allowed anywhere inside the Haram. Photographs are strictly forbidden. If you are caught taking a picture, the camera will be taken from you and the film destroyed.

We go inside and walk through several sections of the mosque. We come to a large courtyard with elegant tenting overhead, which allows in sunlight and fresh air. The Persian carpets, the marble pillars, the intricate architecture, stretch for what seems forever into the distance.

We come to a clearing where several women are sitting on the carpeted floor. Some are making *salaah* – performing prayers – others are reading from their books and reciting. A double row of *zamzam* barrels with paper cups lines the aisle.

We settle ourselves for a few minutes in this area and perform two *rak'ahs* – two sets of prayers with two prostrations – for the mosque, and separate prayers for our children, our deceased parents, and for the Nabi Muhammad (pbuh). Gadidja then leads us up to the front. The whole point is to get to the screen, which is as close as you can get to the back of the Sacred Chamber. To get to it, however, you have to manoeuvre yourself between hundreds of women of all nationalities, who are all vying for a spot where they'll try to perform two *rak'ahs*. The female *asgharis* in their black cloaks are plentiful and vigilant. If they see you standing around, they move you along. 'La! ... La!' they wave you off with a black-gloved hand. The idea is to do what you have

to do and give other people a chance. But people pay scant attention and some of them are prodded along.

I manage to get up to the front, and make two *rak'ahs*. While my head is on the ground, someone tries to clamber over me, and I get a toe in the head. I pay no attention. As long as I'm praying, the *asgharis* can't chase me off. I'm welled up with emotion. The experience is bewildering. But through my emotion and tears, I'm also angry. Why did the Arabs change the rules to prevent women from coming in at the same entrance as the men and from viewing the front of the *kab'r*? Why can't we also see where the Prophet (pbuh) is buried? Twenty years ago, both men and women were able to view the gravesite. Where I was standing now, with my head almost touching the screen, I was at the side of the *kab'r* of the Caliph Umr, but there was no opening for me to put my head through and peer sideways and catch a glimpse. Still, I was a few feet away from the grave of the Prophet (pbuh) whose name was included in my five daily prayers. I was here, in Medina, in his mosque.

All about me women scramble to get a spot. All they want is a few moments to greet the Nabi, the Prophet (pbuh), and make their supplications and pleas. Some are touching the screen and then rubbing their faces with their hands. To do this with a sacred chamber or structure is frowned upon, but people are overwhelmed by being so close to the grave. And there's a certain decorum to be observed by the men when standing in front of the grille door concealing the grave. They are not to stand close to it. They would not have stood close to the Prophet (pbuh) or touched him during his lifetime; why would they want to do so now?

A few facts about the Sacred Chamber – the room in which the Holy Prophet (pbuh) used to live with his wife Aisha – will make it easier to understand the layout in the mosque.

When the Prophet's Mosque was being built, two huts were also being constructed for his wives Aisha and Sawdah. More huts were built as the number of wives increased. All these huts were adjacent to the mosque and their doors opened into the mosque. Each hut consisted of a room, the walls built with unbaked mud bricks and the roof covered with the branches of palm trees. When Omar bin Abdul Aziz expanded the Prophet's Mosque, he included in it all the huts except Aisha's.

As described in the Bukhari source of the traditions, Aisha said, 'The Prophet Muhammad said during his illness before his death, "Where will I stay tonight? Where am I supposed to be tomorrow?" All his wives very willingly agreed to let him stay in my chamber during his final illness. He passed away when his head was in my lap. He was buried in my room.'

There are different theories about the relative positions of the graves of the Prophet Muhammad (pbuh) and his two Companions resting in the Sacred Chamber. The version preferred by most scholars is that the grave closest to the southern wall of the Sacred Chamber is that of the Prophet (pbuh). The grave of the Caliph Abu Bak'r – the father of Aisha – is slightly to the north of the Prophet's grave (pbuh), and in such a way that the head of Abu Bak'r is in line with the shoulders of the Prophet (pbuh). Slightly north of it is the grave of the Caliph Omar, whose head is in line with the shoulders of Abu Bak'r.

The other Companions never placed bricks or other materials on the three graves. There are several references to indicate that the graves were 'neither very high above the ground, nor totally level with the ground. It was covered with a reddish colour earth.'

A renowned scholar, Samhoudi, mentioned in *Vafa-ul-Vafa* that the walls of the Sacred Chamber were remodelled in 878 AH. He had the privilege and honour of entering the Sacred Chamber during the repairs.

He said, 'As I entered the Sacred Chamber, I found a very delicate fragrance there. I offered salutation to the Prophet (pbuh) and his Companions. Then I focused my attention on the condition of the graves so that I could describe it fully to others. All three graves were almost even to the ground level. At one place there was a slight rise above the ground level. It was probably Omar's grave. The graves were definitely covered by ordinary earth.'

Perhaps this was what my friend meant when he said, 'It was rural in there.' Perhaps he had seen the red earth, or perhaps not. Maybe he had only imagined he'd seen it. It was difficult to look through the grille when you were being moved along.

I move out of the way to give other women a chance. The women standing and sitting and praying are of many different nationalities. The Turks are in abundance with their plain beige dresses and suits, the Indonesians in bright green head bands and white robes, the Indian women in maroon-red scarves and other bright colours, the Malaysians in various shades of green; and there are women from a host of other countries, including the local Arab women in their black *abayahs,* with just their eyes showing.

I move to the back and find another spot in the mosque, where I make two *rak'ahs* for my deceased parents and two *rak'ahs* for my children, Zaida and Faramarz. I am hardly back at the hotel, when it's time to take ablution again and head back to the mosque for *thuh'r* prayers.

Day 4 – Friday December 17th 2004

By our second day in Medina, we're getting used to the routine, but are jetlagged from the long trip. Our daily schedule is hectic. At five in the morning we're up. When the *athan* – the call to prayer – sounds in Cape Town, it means that it's time to perform your *salaah*. When it sounds in Medina, it gives you fifteen minutes to get to the mosque, when a second *athan* will be heard and prayers will start.

We have six people in our two rooms, and one toilet. All of us have to take ablution before we go to mosque. For the first two days, we try to wait for one another to go together to the mosque, but as we get used to our surroundings, we no longer wait and instead go off on our own. More and more people are arriving from other countries.

The Haram is full. You have to get to the mosque earlier to get a spot.

I'm amazed at the change within myself. In Cape Town, I had gone to see a psychologist to deal with my fear of crowds, and here I am, leaving the others behind, in the midst of a horde of people, feeling quite at ease. I pray in different parts of the mosque, and don't favour only one spot. I especially like praying outside on the marble *mataff*. It's my belief that the more places I pray in, the greater the likelihood that my steps will cross those of the Prophet's wives and his Companions, and of the Prophet himself (pbuh). All of the mosque and the precinct surrounding it had been their playground. I can imagine a dusty path and camels and horses. I can see the women cooking and the children playing about their skirts. I can visualise the Prophet (pbuh) speaking to a beggar or a merchant or a king. I can

even imagine what the Prophet (pbuh) might've looked like, but will not think too hard about it in case I build up an incorrect image in my head. But if I didn't know if Muhammad Mustafa (pbuh) was ruddy-complexioned or dark, or had curly or woolly hair, I knew what he'd carried in his heart for his Lord.

It's Friday. We know the mosque will be packed for *jum'ah*, the midday prayers. Still, we have no idea of the multitudes that will flock to the mosque. We had noticed the crowds getting thicker with new *hujaj* who were all coming to Medina first before going on to Mecca, but we are still shocked by the sheer number of people who show up.

'This is just the tip of the iceberg,' someone says. 'Wait till we get to Mecca.'

The hour of *jum'ah* arrives. All of Medina shows up, including the residents. We arrive early, but don't even reach the door of the mosque. The rows stretch down the *mataff*. We put down our *muslahs* where we

can, ensuring that we join up and continue the row.

After prayers, the others go out shopping for presents. I return to the hotel to write. This isn't the kind of book that allows you to wait until after hajj to write up your impressions. I want to be in the moment to report exactly how I feel. I also can't spend too much time at it as I don't want it interfering with my hajj. But hajj is for five days only, and still five weeks away.

Two hours later, before *asr* prayers, the roommates return. They've been out shopping for scarves, and come home with some beautiful silk, chiffon and coloured ones. Shopping has become the favoured activity of the women on the floor. Everywhere you look, they are laden with bags – shopping and more shopping – and still they are sitting on their beds with long lists of all those cousins and aunts and nephews and nieces they have to buy for. I'm not a shopper. I went out once to buy a few robes and prayer mats, and two dresses for special occasions, and that was it.

As to the people filling up the streets of Medina, most of them are *hujaj*. You can spot them by their headbands, wristbands, bags, style of clothing, different languages. They move in groups, up and down the same roads, back and forth to the mosque. Medina is the place for pilgrims before hajj. Between two and three million people will pass through by the time hajj is over at the end of January.

The residents are different. You notice immediately that the local women are conspicuously absent from the streets. The men are the ones you see. They serve in the shops and restaurants and work in offices. Only men drive cars. Women stay at home and look after the

children. At the mosque, you may see the Arab women in their black *abayahs* with their toddlers. During *salaah*, when they have to put those babies down, or leave them in the care of an older sibling, you will hear a cacophony of cries. But the women don't look at you, and they don't talk. They're not friendly. Unlike the *hujaj*, who are there for the same reason as you, they do not exchange pleasantries while you are sitting next to each other on your mats. This is their city; we are the visitors, taking over their streets, filling up the mosque. The things that we stand in awe of, seeing them for the first time, are no longer of wonder to them. We come to Medina with a fresh eye and passion.

Still, you will see older Arab women selling things on the street. Usually they are wearing their black cloaks and headscarves with only their eyes showing, and have all their goods displayed on flat little wooden wagons on wheels, with long handles, which they use

to pull the wagons when they move off.

I have been walking around Medina with a camera, stopping people, asking if it's all right to snap them. The men, for the most part, are receptive: they're not used to strange women speaking to them. There's no dating in Medina. No cinemas. No places to which young men and women may go together. Going together is not an option. A man sees a woman he likes, he speaks to his father, who speaks to the girl's father, and a match is made. So entering a shop, striking up a conversation in a language I can't speak, waving a camera, is a novelty. Perhaps they're too surprised to say no. Or perhaps they just like being photographed. And they know some English.

'Where you from?'

'Sud Afrika. Mandela.'

'Aah ... Mandela. Sud Afrika.'

And they pose for you. And laugh. They're friendly, but not the Arab women with their portable wagons. If they catch you pointing your camera at them, they screech 'La! La!' and they wave you off.

An Arab woman selling dresses and metres of material all neatly folded on her little wooden platform sees me about to photograph her, and gets angry. I snap her anyway, and then later come back and inspect the goods on her wagon. I see a dark-green brocaded dress I like.

'How much?'

She holds up ten black-gloved fingers. Her lips don't move.

'Eight?'

Dark, kohl-rimmed eyes stare me down.

I take out ten rials. She takes the money, and puts the dress in a plastic packet. Not a smile, nor a word of thanks.

By the time I'd been in Medina a week, walking up and down to the Haram past the bazaars five times a day, I had got to know many of the shop owners. 'Photo! Photo!' they would call out at me, and

smile. I would smile back. I was a foreign woman. Foreign women had strange practices. They asked questions, they talked to strangers. They took photos of other men.

But it's a man's world, to be sure. You see the young Arab men all day, lolling about, standing talking with friends: the contract workers from Pakistan, Egypt and other countries are the ones who do the cleaning up and work in the hotels. Men have their friendships with men. It's not unusual to see them walking in the street, holding hands. I ask one of the Arabs I'd photographed in Foreign Exchange why men hold hands with other men in the street. He smiles, finding the question strange. 'Is okay,' he says. 'Is friends.'

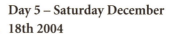

Day 5 – Saturday December 18th 2004

Masjid Qiblataine

As usual, we get up before dawn to go to the mosque, have our breakfast afterwards at the hotel at 6.15, and then go to our room either for a nap – we get very little sleep – or to discuss what we're doing that day. This morning, however, the group has a tour planned in our bus, and right after breakfast we are taken to a few places of historical interest in Medina.

We visit Quba Mosque, the first mosque in Medina, the foundation of which was laid by the Prophet (pbuh) himself. We also visit Masjid Qiblataine – the mosque with two *qiblas*. The significance of this mosque is that during the time of the Prophet (pbuh), one had to face Al Aqsar in Jerusalem while praying. While the Prophet (pbuh) was at the mosque performing the *zuhr* prayers, revelation came that he had to change the *qibla* (direction of prayer) towards Mecca. The mosque still has the two *qiblas*, but prayers are performed only in the direction of Mecca. We stop at both mosques and perform voluntary prayers.

Then we proceed to Jab'l Uhud – the mountainous terrain where the Battle of Uhud had taken place. The Prophet Muhammad (pbuh) set out with one thousand men, one third of whom turned back home after travelling part of the way towards Mount Uhud under the influence of Abdullah bin Ubay. The Prophet (pbuh) proceeded with the remaining men until he pitched camp at the trail of Mount Uhud – putting the mountain behind them, and facing the idolators. He assigned 50 archers under the command of Abdullah bin Jubair to man a small strategic foothill, and commanded them not to leave their position under any circumstances. He said, 'Even if you see us being killed, do not come to our aid, and if you see us taking booty, do not take part.'

The following morning, the Prophet (pbuh) mobilised his army. The Quraysh – 3 000 in number – also readied themselves. The two armies went into battle. The Muslims initially gained the upper hand, and were victorious; the Quraysh fled. When the archers saw the fleeing Quraysh, some of them left the foothill which the Prophet (pbuh) had commanded them to guard, and went for the booty. The Quraysh emerged from behind the foothill and killed the remaining archers. The Muslims were surrounded by the Quraysh, and the Prophet himself (pbuh) suffered injury. They lost the battle.

It was after this battle, as a result of which many men had lost their lives, and women and children were left destitute, that the revelation came that a man could have more than one wife. The revelation was not without condition - that if a man could not be fair, he must only have one.

The last stop is at an out-of-the-way factory at which all kinds of dates are sold. The Prophet (pbuh) used to love dates and often lived on nothing but dates and goat milk. A tiny black date a little bigger than an olive, called *ajwa*, is said to have been a special favourite. There is *hadith* that if you eat seven of these dates early in the morning, no poisons will harm your body that day.

I buy two kilos of dates to take home with me.

Days 6 to 9 – December 19th to 22nd 2004

Essentially, every day in Medina is the same. You wake up before dawn, take ablution, go to the mosque, have breakfast, go shopping, take a nap, take ablution, go to the mosque, have lunch, take ablution, go to the mosque, have a rest, take ablution, go to the mosque, walk around for an hour, take ablution, go to the mosque. Your whole day revolves around prayer. The moment you hear the *athan*, you drop whatever you're doing and you're gone.

By this stage of our visit it is no longer practical to wait for the *athan* before leaving to go to mosque. By the time you hear it, the mosque has already filled up with people who have gone an hour before the time. This morning at dawn is the first time I try to get inside after several days of praying outside on the *mataff*, but even though I get there at five, there is no place anywhere to squeeze myself in. An Indian woman takes pity and moves to her left so that I can get in next to her. I feel hemmed in and claustrophobic, but am grateful for the spot.

It's our last day in Medina. We have to bid salaam to the Nabi Muhammad (pbuh). After breakfast I go back to the mosque to make final *salaahs*.

Inside Mecca

Day 10 - Thursday December 23rd 2004

The day starts with great expectation. We're going to Mecca. Medina was a preparation, a build-up for what was to come. Medina has nothing directly to do with hajj, but Medina and Mecca are connected by virtue of revelation – one being the Prophet's birthplace (pbuh), the other the place where he died – and it makes sense for pilgrims to visit Medina first. Mecca is where we are now headed. Our pilgrimage has now officially started. We get up as usual before dawn, go to mosque, have breakfast, and at 8.30 meet outside the hotel. From here we go as a group, led by Sheikh Gabriels, for the last time to bid farewell to the Holy Prophet (pbuh).

As we are men and women together, we don't go inside the mosque, but rather to the men's entrance where we'd been the first day. We stand back at a distance of about a hundred feet to catch a glimpse of the *kab'r* of the Nabi (pbuh), and his two Caliphs.

Sheikh Gabriels leads a short prayer and we say farewell. We cry and hug one another. We're sad when we drive out of the city in the bus and leave the Prophet's Mosque behind. We don't know when we will see it again, if ever. We will have only our memories of the place where God's last prophet (pbuh) lived his last years and died.

We're in *ihram* now to enter Mecca for the first time: the women in white robes and petticoats and long white pants, and the men in two pieces of unstitched towelling – one for around the waist, and one draped over one shoulder. We have already taken our *ghus'l*, a special ablution after our shower, and will stop at Bir Ali, which is the *miqat* for us to perform the  prayer to don the *ihram*. We are now unable to scratch ourselves, swat an insect or behave in a disorderly way. We are in *ihram* because once we enter Mecca we will perform our *umrah*, which is part of the hajj.

I am in the bus now, scribbling in a small diary. Three hours have passed. The sun is past the halfway mark, the day is declining. The steady drone of the bus puts everyone to sleep.

I look out the window. The landscape is fickle and ever-changing. We pass a grove of palm trees. The land changes to dusty, yellow rock. Here and there are a few sparse bushes. Three camels are standing close to a fence. Then the land changes again, to huge mounds of black stone. The sun has no mercy in this part of the world: everything is burnt black. But we are lucky to be here in winter, in 30-degree weather. I look out through the front of the bus. The blue asphalt road snakes onward. We cut through a range of mountains, and come out the other side. There's life again: a petrol station with a few faded streamers, a stone dwelling with palm fronds for a roof. Then it all fades away again to desolation. Where are the sand dunes of Arabia I'd seen so often on the big screen?

It is getting dark. We have been on the road for six hours. The bus slows and we pull into a rough patch of pebbled driveway: we have reached a restaurant. We get out and stretch our legs. We are hungry, and go in, but it is dark inside and we can't initially make out the food through the two glass counters. One is filled with cabbages and tomatoes. The other has stainless steel containers of hot food.

'Light ... light,' I say to one of the men behind the counter.

'Is coming,' he smiles. 'Five minoots.'

We wait. There is a generator problem. Finally, the lights go on. We can see what is in the pots: there are beans and a vegetable curry. We decide on roast chicken and Egyptian kebab, based on what we see on other people's plates. The food comes on big platters of yellow sweet rice, with half a roast chicken or kebabs on top. We are going to eat the Arab way, with everyone seated at the table around the two plates, dipping in with our hands.

Having been married to an Iranian in Canada, I am used to mince kebab on the flat skewer, but one of the men in our party thinks the meat has a wild taste.

'It can't be beef,' he says. 'Hulle gee vir ons kameel.' They're giving us camel.

We laugh. I don't think it is camel meat, but ask the proprietor on the way out.

'Cow,' he says emphatically. 'Not camel.'

We're off again. We arrive at the outskirts of Mecca at 10.30 at night. The bus climbs steadily higher. We have been sitting on the bus for more than ten hours and are tired and groggy. Even so, I am alert enough to note that Mecca is different from Medina. Medina has serenity: it is calm and tranquil. Mecca throbs with life.

The bus reaches the top of the hill and dips down into the valley. The streets are well-lit and busy — lined with apartments and monstrous hotels and buildings. But the first thing you notice is the bustle. There

are people everywhere, even though it is after ten at night. And Mecca is old. Medina has an old Medina and a modern Medina, and you can see where the one ends and the other begins. Mecca is chock-full of open air markets, stalls, carts and bazaars, all crammed right in between huge modern buildings. It is both old and new, dilapidated and vibrant.

The Holy City has approximately 50 names: Mecca, Bakkah, Al-Balad, Al-Qaryah and many others. In Arabic, the word 'Balad' means 'the main city'. Mecca sits in a bowl. At the lowest point of this depression is the Grand Mosque – al Haram – and in the centre of the mosque, in the courtyard, is the Kab'ah – the Sacred House of God.

The Kab'ah was first built by the angels, then rebuilt by Adam, then built again by Abraham with his son Ishmail, then by the Quraysh – witnessed by the Prophet Muhammad (pbuh) when he was 25 years old – and for the fifth time by Ibn Az-Zubair.

Much of hajj centres on Abraham, Hagar and Ishmail. When Ishmail was born to Hagar, Abraham's first wife Sarah became intensely jealous of Hagar and asked Abraham to take her away. God revealed to Abraham that he should take Hagar and her son to Mecca. Abraham did so and, on one of his visits to see them, he found Ishmail sharpening an arrow beneath a tree.

'O Ishmail,' he said, 'Allah has commanded me to do something.'

'Do what your Lord has commanded you to do,' Ishmail responded.

Abraham asked whether he would help him. Ishmail said yes.

'God has commanded me to build a house here,' Abraham said, and pointed to a small rise in the land. Here they started to lay the foundation of the House. Ishmail brought the stones and Abraham started to build. As the structure got higher, Ishmail brought a stone for his father to stand on as he worked, and handed up the stones for building to him. The stone on which Abraham stood is called Al-Maqam. His footprints on the stone – faded away with time and much rubbing and touching – are today preserved in a glass case a few feet from the Kab'ah. When pilgrims circumambulate the Sacred House, they pass by it seven times during their *tawaaf*.

Al-Maqam, containing Abraham's footprint

Abraham is considered to be the first idol smasher, and chastised his own father for worshipping the moon and the stars. At a time when people were worshipping many gods, he submitted completely to the One God.

Some centuries later, Muhammad Mustafa is born in Mecca. Orphaned as a young child, he is cared for by his uncle, Abu Lahab. At the age of 25, he is employed as a merchant by the wealthy and widowed Khadidja. The working relationship is a good one and Khadidja asks him to marry her. She is fifteen years older than he is. Muhammad accepts. They have a good life together; Muhammad has no other wife during her lifetime.

At the age of 40, on one of his spiritual retreats in the mountains around Mecca, Muhammad is in a cave and is visited by the Angel Gabriel, who commands him to read.

'*Iqraa!*' the Angel commands.

Muhammad is terrified. He cannot read.

'*Read in the name of Thy Lord who has created you ... created you from a clot of blood!*'

The Angel had him in its grip, and commanded him to repeat after him. Muhammad did so. Then the presence left. Muhammad thought something was wrong with him, and ran from the cave to his wife, Khadidja, who put a blanket around his shoulders and comforted him. That was the first Revelation, and the beginning of his prophethood.

The holy Prophet Muhammad (pbuh)

was born during Jahiliyah, the Age of Ignorance, when the Arabs used to bury their female infants and worship idols. The Kab'ah had 360 idols around it. At the end of his mission, at age 63, after 23 years of revelation, the Prophet Muhammad (pbuh) had brought a spirituality to the Arabs uniquely suited to their own traditions, and destroyed all the idols, re-establishing the monotheism started by Abraham.

There is an interesting story set during the time the Kab'ah was rebuilt for the fourth time. Muhammad (pbuh) was then only 25. His mission hadn't begun yet. The Kab'ah at that time was a structure of stones built without mortar, no higher than a man. The Quraysh wanted to rebuild it and give it a roof. A ship belonging to a Roman merchant had been wrecked off the coast of Jeddah and smashed to pieces. They took its wood and prepared to make a roof. Then the Quraysh started to collect stones, each tribe gathering stones by themselves. They started to build and continued until they reached the point where the Black Stone – Haj'r Al-Aswad – which had first been laid into the foundation of the Kab'ah by the prophet Abraham, could be put back in place. The problem was that everyone wanted to have the honour of lifting it up and putting it in place. The dispute lasted for days. They were about to fight when an old man said, 'O Quraysh, come to an agreement concerning that over which you are disputing, and let the first man who enters through the gate of this mosque decide the matter for you.'

The first man to come through the gate was the young Muhammad. When they saw him, they said, 'This is Al-Amin (the trustworthy one). We agree to accept Muhammad's decision.'

Muhammad listened to the dispute and then asked them to bring him a cloak. He placed the cloak on the ground, picked up the Black Stone and placed it on the cloak.

'Let each tribe take an edge of the cloak, and all of you lift it up together.'

They did this, and construction continued.

So we are finally in Mecca. We have come to perform hajj. Hajj literally means 'to travel towards God'. It also implies exertion to master the self. Hajj has specific obligations attached to it, and has as much to do with Abraham, Hagar and Ishmail as it has to do with the holy Prophet Muhammad (pbuh), who was born in Mecca, and who died in Medina.

We arrive at the hotel, Al-Kareem. The bus stops and four young men get on. One hands out cold bottles of *zamzam* water, another gives us a date biscuit, another offers a plate of dates. We get out. We are in the middle of a narrow street with people teeming all around us: vendors, pilgrims, tradesmen, women sitting on blankets on the ground selling nuts or prayer mats or robes – all just a few hundred feet away from the Grand Mosque.

We go up to our room on the tenth floor. We have to freshen up and be back in the lobby within half an hour with the rest of the group. The first thing we have to do upon entering Mecca, in *ihram*, is to perform the *umrah* and the *saee*.

We get upstairs to the tenth floor to check into our room and find ourselves in a room smaller than the one we had in Medina: four beds in a very small space and a tiny window which opens up onto a wall. You can't tell whether it's day or night. There isn't room to swing a cat. On the other hand, it's neat, and the bathroom has a regular toilet. But how are four women going to live in this tiny room for five weeks? We have no time to answer that question now. We put down our bags and take our ablutions. We are tired. It is after 11 p.m. What we have to do next will take at least three hours, depending on the crowds we're going to encounter at the Grand Mosque.

We go downstairs. Sheikh Gabriels, bareheaded now, with a long piece of towelling draped around his waist, and another slung over his shoulder, leads the group to the mosque. I am apprehensive and wonder what my reaction will be when I see the Kab'ah for the first time. Will it exceed my reaction when I first set eyes on the Prophet's Mosque?

We walk up to the Haram from the hotel. For the first hundred yards or so the road is cobbled and sandy; right next to our hotel there is construction in progress. There are no cars, except for a huge yellow bulldozer. The road is filled with people even at this late time of night. The stalls are open. The vendors are plying their trade.

We follow our leader up to the mosque. We have started our chant, '*Labaik, lasharikala kalaka labaik* …' O, Lord, here we are …

We walk halfway around the outside of the Haram, go down a flight of steps and enter the mosque. We come into the courtyard, and there it is, the huge black silk-covered cube. I cannot believe that I am standing in front of the Kab'ah. How many pictures I've seen, how much I've heard and read about it. Every day I have positioned my prayer mat facing in its direction. And here I am.

Sheikh Gabriels makes a *duah*. I am crying now, trying not to be heard. We move forward to join the pilgrims making their circuits around the Sacred House. We start at the Black Stone, keeping close together, and we chant. We progress around once, twice, until finally we have made seven circuits. There are a lot of people: the crowd is a moving wheel of human beings. We manage to come close to the wall, but never near to the Black Stone. There's a knot of people shoving in front of it: it's impossible to push through, especially for a woman. We know that we might never have the opportunity to touch it. The *tawaaf* has taken 50 minutes. We go off to the side and perform *salaah*. We have now performed *umrah*.

Next is the ritual relating to Abraham, Hagar and Ishmail. When Abraham took Hagar into the desert and left her there with Ishmail, Hagar soon ran out of water, and ran to and fro between the hills of Safa and Marwa to look for water for her infant son. It was during this time that a spring of water – *Zamzam* – gushed forth.

This ground, between the two hills where Hagar ran in search of water, has to be covered by the pilgrim seven times, and is called *saee*. The *saee* and the *tawaaf* have to be performed by every pilgrim when they enter Mecca.

We follow Sheikh Gabriels back inside the mosque, where there is a very long, wide corridor with people walking up one side and down the other, with a barrier in the middle. The corridor is packed with bodies clothed in white. We start walking, reciting all the time as we walk. When we come to the end of the corridor, the ground slopes up and we are standing on a hill. We repeat the walk down the other side, where we also come to a hill. We walk seven times between these two hills. By the time we are finished, it is two in the morning. We are done. We have performed *umrah* and *saee*. We go to the row of *zamzam* tanks for a drink. The water is cool and refreshing. These tanks of water are everywhere in the Haram, even in the Prophet's Mosque in Medina. This water is not for sale, but is bottled and given away free. *Zamzam* is said to possess special properties, and many people swear that they have been cured by it. It is good-tasting and safe to drink. Water is pumped from the well and then treated with a series of sand filters and microfilters, as well as ultraviolet disinfection – and then stored in underground storage tanks. *Hujaj* take several litres home with them. It is a special treat to offer someone a drink of *zamzam*.

Performing saee

Day 11 – Friday December 24th 2004

After a few hours' sleep we are up again to perform *fajr* prayers at the mosque. We wake up to our cramped space: four suitcases, four overnight bags. Out of the overnight bags come toothbrushes and creams and lotions and bottles. Robes and underclothing come out of the suitcases. There is no place to put the bags except under our beds, which means that we have to take out everything we need before we put them away again. The cupboard has four small compartments for our personal items and there are only three hangers. It isn't long before there's grumpiness in the camp. But we remind ourselves why we're here: we can't afford to get upset with each other. So we rearrange the beds. We agree to keep the bathroom spick and span and dry. There's a communal kitchen and we take turns making something to eat and washing the dishes. Still, we have five weeks looming ahead of us. The weather is hot. We're all menopausal.

Back home in South Africa, it is the day before Christmas. In Mecca, we are gearing up for *jum'ah* prayers. We leave almost half an hour before the *athan* sounds. But the streets are jammed with pilgrims. When we arrive at the Haram, the *mataff* has filled up, and it's impossible to get inside.

It's our intention to go and *tawaaf* around the Kab'ah at eleven o'clock that night when the *zahmah* is not so full. I am tired, and would prefer to go in the morning at around seven. There are still a lot of people then, but it's not packed. Still, I am thinking of the press of the crowds, and don't want to go by myself: it's not wise in any event to do so. All pilgrims receive a leather wristband when they arrive at their hotels in Mecca. On it, in Arabic, is the name of your group and the hotel you are staying at. This is to identify you in the event you get lost, or die when there is no one with you.

Day 12 – Saturday December 25th 2004

At seven in the morning, one of my roommates and I go to the Haram to do a *tawaaf*. The Haram is full, but the crowd around the Kab'ah looks manageable. We manoeuvre our way into the wheel, holding onto one another. Soon we  find ourselves in the middle of the throng, and move out to the edge. We do the first circuit, then the second, then the third, the wheel of humanity swelling all the time. At one point, we manage to come up to the wall of the Kab'ah, and even manage to make two *rak'ahs* at the spot where Abraham was to have sacrificed his infant son and where the Angel Gabriel appeared.

Ghjr'l Ishmail is a semi-circle in front of one part of the Kab'ah where the biers containing the deceased are placed during prayer time. *Janazah salaah* is recited at the end, and you have a chance to pray for the dead. The biers are then lifted and taken away to the cemetery. At every *waq't* so far there have been one or more deceased.

Eventually, 40 minutes later, we have completed seven circuits. We have done it all by ourselves. By the time we're finished, the crowd performing *tawaaf* has evolved to more than double its size. We feel wonderful, as well as mightily relieved that we have managed to do a *tawaaf*. We plan to perform it again at eleven o'clock that evening.

11.00 p.m. I stay in and don't go with the others. I'm reluctant to break with my routine, and am the first one in bed, and the first one up, at 5.00 a.m. After a full schedule of going back and forth to the mosque five times a day, while also trying to keep a record of events, I am too tired to be adventurous at this time of the night.

Day 13 – Sunday December 26th 2004

The day starts as usual. Mosque, breakfast, writing. After lunch, when we go for our *asr* prayers, the throng of people in the street seems to have come to a standstill and you can't move. As we inch forward, we see that a large part of the road has been cordoned off. We all look to discover what it is in this sealed-off area that warrants such a crowd. And there we see a single sandal and a wooden shutter, in splintered pieces. We look up. The shutter has blown off the window of the hotel above. They're investigating: this is the crime scene. I am sure that with thousands of people blocking the road going to mosque, when the shutter blew off it must have struck someone on the head, possibly killing them.

After writing this last paragraph, I go downstairs to buy dates from a vendor. Five feet from the hotel door, there are several carts with delicious fruit and another with dates. There's no one in attendance at the date cart so I turn to the man selling fruit at the next stall and motion with my hands to ask him where the date vendor is. He points to an Arab in a red headscarf and a jacket, rolled up in a carpet on a bench. He doesn't want to wake him up, and decides to serve me himself.

'How much a kilo?' I ask.

He shows with his hands, fifteen rials.

I hand him a ten. 'Half a kilo, please.'

He weighs the dates. They are the black, chewy ones that the Prophet (pbuh) used to favour. He hands me the dates, and takes the note to the man on the bench. He manages to wake him up and get me two rials change. The Arab on the bench goes back to sleep. He is not worried about his dates: his dates are safe. A pilgrim won't steal. His hajj won't be any good if he does such a thing.

Later in the day, I decide to try to find out in which hotel my cousin Mareldia is staying. When you are so far away from home, you yearn for a relative. Mareldia and I became close during the previous three years, after my mother had a stroke and came to live with me. She had helped me many times with my mother.

But trying to find a pilgrim without knowing the name of the group she is travelling with is virtually impossible in a city hosting a couple of million pilgrims. I contact SAHUC, the South African Council for Hajj and Umrah. They take her name and make no promises that they will find her. They are not computerised, and 7 500 hujaj have come in from South Africa. Still, the next day I get a call. They have found her details. She is staying at the Al Safaar Hotel off Samia Street.

I ask my roommates for directions – they have been to Samia Street the day before. I go in search of the hotel by myself, and find it almost

on top of the hill on the other side of the Haram. I go inside and ask if they can tell me what floor Mareldia is staying on. But the names of pilgrims are not kept in registers: pilgrims are registered under a group and the Arabs at the desk can't speak English and are of no assistance. I go back outside and

find a woman who tells me that all the South Africans are on the tenth floor. I go back inside and take the lift up. There are 24 rooms. I start to knock on doors. No one seems to be home. But on the ninth or the tenth try, a man answers. What are the chances, I wonder, with 24 rooms on the floor that he would know how I can find my cousin? I explain who I am and who I'm looking for. He's a big man, in a white robe. Indian.

'Yes,' he beams. 'They are right next door.'

I thank him and go next door. I knock and knock. No one is in. I go back to the Indian man's door, and ask whether he has a pen and a piece of paper. While he fetches it, I catch a glimpse of his room. His wife and a young child are sitting on the bed. Their room is even more crowded than ours. I am suddenly grateful for the little room we have at Al-Kareem, and for our communal kitchen. The man has his entire store of food on the table.

I write a note for my cousin and leave it under the door. The same night she phones me. She has been in the Haram all day, praying, making a *tawaaf* and reading from her books. She would like to see me, but can't do so the following morning, as they will be opening the door of the Kab'ah – she witnessed this during her last hajj a few years ago and wants to be there at six in the morning to get a spot. I promise to meet her at the green light before six.

Day 14 – Monday December 27th 2004

I get up as usual with the others to go to the mosque. But everyone, it seems, has heard the news that the door of the Kab'ah will be opened, and the mosque swarms with people. When prayers are over, I make my way to the place where my cousin said she would be, but it is so crowded that I can't even get a spot from which to look for her.

I return to the hotel. One of the men in our party returns a few hours later from the Haram and makes us all jealous. He had gone for a *tawaaf* right after *fajr*, and the *zahmah* was so full, he said, that they had moved forward in inches around the Kab'ah. Then the army arrived, and the king, and a string of dignitaries, and they put a little ramp – like they do for passengers to board a plane – in front of the Kab'ah door, for the king.

'I was on the other side of the Kab'ah. But the people pushed so that they pushed me right in front of the door, and I saw everything.'

We can't believe that he has been so fortunate as to witness such a thing. With thousands of people all pushing to be in front of the door, he had ended up in exactly the right spot.

'What did you see?' we all ask.

'Well, the king first walked in. They shone a big light through the door, and I saw a piece of wood – a rack or trellis thing, like they have in the Haram, on which they put the Qur'ans. There's nothing inside, but the wall is a kind of green colour. Then someone went in, and came out on top of the roof, and cleaned up there. There must be a ladder inside.'

'Did anyone clean inside?' I ask.

'Yes. The king took a broom – a riete besem – and kind of swept a little in the front there.'

I am envious, but know that even if I had been with my cousin, we wouldn't have had the view he had had. The cleaning of the Kab'ah is an event. In the next few weeks, when the pilgrims perform hajj, the black silk cloth covering of the Kab'ah will also be removed, and a new one put on.

After lunch, the others go out to shop. I stay in and write. They don't come back to the hotel, and I go by myself to the mosque for *asr* prayers. When prayers are over, I decide to check out the *zahmah* around the Kab'ah. If it is not too full, I will attempt a *tawaaf* on my own. But I reach the courtyard and all I can see is a sea of people. I feel panic as I visualise myself in the thick of that crowd. I decide not to go but the anxiety lingers. When I come back to the mosque for the sunset prayers, I realise that I am not wearing my wristband. I am alone in the mosque, and feel suddenly hot. My chest feels a little tight. I'm aware that I'm feeling panicky. But these are not new feelings; they're from long ago. I know I will be all right. I finish my prayers and walk back to the hotel. I go to bed. We are going to have a very early day the next day, and have to be up and waiting down in the foyer at 5.00 a.m. We're going on a tour.

Day 15 – Tuesday December 28th 2004

At the appointed time, we are all in the foyer. It is still dark outside. But the streets are alive with residents and pilgrims and vendors who never seem to sleep. Two buses are waiting. Our first stop is a very special place: Jab'l Nur, the mountain where the holy Prophet Muhammad (pbuh) received the first Revelation.

I am excited about this. I had seen pictures of the cave where the Prophet (pbuh) had sat when the Angel Gabriel came to him, but had always wanted to go there myself. In the pictures, I couldn't see enough of the interior of the cave. I could see that it was small, just big enough to stand up in and pray, but I could not see enough detail to satisfy me. I would finally have occasion to visit this most holy site myself, and imagine how it might all have happened. I could never get out of my mind the image of a bright presence commanding the Prophet Muhammad (pbuh) to read.

First, though, we have to go to the mosque at the bottom of the hill to make *faj'r salaah*. Going to the Haram for this *salaah* would've made us late to start climbing Jab'l Nur. We don't want to be up on the summit in the heat.

The bus stops. We get out and walk up a steep little street. The

mosque is small. We perform *salaah* and then meet outside. We walk across to the next street and start the trek up. The road up to the base of the mountain is so steep that it reminds me of Leeuwen Street in Cape Town, only worse. It's cool still, and dark. We walk up against a slight wind. The

group soon breaks up as those with more stamina and leg power move up ahead. I'm in the middle group, stopping every ten feet. My one-hour walks back home aren't helping me here. I'm not one to go hiking uphill. Still, I get to the foot of the mountain. We're high up now. I can't afford to look back down at the city below. I have a fear of heights.

I put my camera in my robe pocket for easy access, say *bismillah*, and start to feel my way upwards over the rocks. I do well. About a quarter of the way up, I take out my camera and make a big mistake by turning around and looking down. I freeze, and have an insane desire

to float downwards. I know it's the force of gravity that I'm responding to. I can't bear to look. I feel dizzy. I remember what someone had told me before leaving home: 'What you are expecting will not happen. And what you don't expect will come about.'

I had not expected that I would have difficulty getting up to Jabl'l Nur. All my fears had to do with crowds and the pelting of the Jamarahs.

I turn around. I can't imagine what will happen if I get all the way to the top, look down, freeze and can't come down. Reluctantly, I hand my camera to a friend and ask her if she can take a few pictures. I go back down, a few inches at a time, and sit with another pilgrim on the steps of a shop and prepare myself for a long wait. As I sit there looking at some of the alleyways and the houses, I wonder where the Prophet Muhammad (pbuh) had lived at the time when he ran to his wife Khadidja in fear. Had it been in this neighbourhood, or far away?

The buildings are old. In between many of them are ruins of still other buildings, which had been built long, long ago. A strange thing I notice, while sitting there, is an Arab coming up the hill in a 4x4 jeep. It is so out of place in this remote spot, with rocks and goats and ruins. What is a vehicle like that doing here?

I see him stop at the foot of the mountain about twenty feet or so from a stall selling drinks. The Arab knows that the pilgrims coming down the mountain will be tired and is there to offer them a lift to the bus. All he does is drive up and down in a 4x4. It's a business.

Hardly twenty minutes later, the woman I'd given my camera to comes down. I am happy to see that she is back so soon.

'Did you get some pictures for me?' I ask.

'No,' she says, leaning with her hands on her knees and gasping. 'My calves just couldn't take it any more. And when I was up there, the wind was so strong and there was just this little step to hang on to. I was scared. I thought I'd better come down.'

I'm glad that I'd turned around, but sad too that I had lost this one superb opportunity to stand inside the cave where the Prophet Muhammad (pbuh) had received his first Revelation. I was missing some special opportunities: first, the door of the Kab'ah being opened, and now this. Still, I was satisfied with the pictures I'd taken so far in Medina and Mecca – not an easy task when you're not allowed to shoot in the vicinity of the Haram, and when people don't want their photos taken. You can get into trouble for taking someone's picture on the street without asking first. The foreigners don't mind but the Arab women, especially, will make a racket if you take a picture of them surreptitiously. And I've taken a few. One woman cackled like an old hen till I'd dodged out of sight.

The others in the group come down after a while, and boast many shots. A lot of them are poses in front of the cave but there are no pictures at all of the inside of the cave. I wonder why people always have to take pictures of themselves in front of historical sites. Do we want to see them, or where they've been?

Our next stop is Mount Rahmah at Mina. And also Arafah. We are seeing the places we will go to before the millions during hajj. The purpose of the visit is to familiarise ourselves, and to take a walk up Mount Rahmah as we won't have the opportunity during hajj. There will be millions of people. And the South African camp is some distance away.

Last, we visit the place where we will pelt the three Jamarahs. In earlier years, they were all on ground level. But owing to the hordes of pilgrims, and the problems with trampling, the Saudis built a bridge over them, and one can now pelt on the ground level as well as on the bridge. They have also extended the width of the Jamarahs so that pilgrims don't have to be right up in front to be able to hit them, making

it easier to extricate oneself from the crowds. It is quiet now, not a scrap of litter or a soul to be seen. It will be a different story during hajj. Not far from the pelting site is a humble little mosque called Masjid Baya. 'Baya' means pledge. It is the mosque where the Ansar gave the pledge of allegiance to the Prophet Muhammad (pbuh). It touches me when I visit a site where some of the old structures remain.

When we reach the hotel, there is a note waiting for me from my cousin. Ten minutes later, she is in our room. I am happy to see her. We go down to the Haram together for *asr* prayers. I ask her whether she wants to go and *tawaaf* afterwards.

'I'm too tired to go at eleven at night with the others,' I add.

'I don't mind,' she says, 'but I go on the next level. It's not so crowded up there.'

'But do you mind going just this once with me on the ground level? I want to get used to the crowds.'

She agrees. After *asr*, she takes out her *kitaab* with the *duahs*, and we head for the Kab'ah. It is full, full, full. People making *tawaaf*. People praying. People sitting on the outer perimeter of the moving wheel. I am aware of feelings of panic, but don't give in to them. Together my cousin and I will make it in this crowd.

We step down onto the *mataff* and walk on the outside. Soon, we are in the thick of things. My cousin is reciting in Arabic from her *kitaab*. I am talking to God. I am pleading for my children's health and spirituality. I am asking for paradise for my parents. I am asking for my own health, and for God to protect me against temptation. *I am here, God. You gave me the invitation to come, here I am. I am your servant. This tawaaf is for me, God. Just for me. Protect me from temptation, and keep me steadfast in my prayers when I return home. Give my children hidaya, and guide them along the right path.*

When Mareldia is finished reading from her *kitaab*, she hands it to me to read the English. I do so. It takes us eight minutes to complete the first circuit. When we near the spot on the brown line – which we can hardly see when we look down because of the bodies pressing in on us from all sides – where we have to raise our hands towards the Kab'ah and say, *Allahu Akbar*, we are moving forward in inches. Immediately we pass the brown line we have some breathing space again – until the next corner, and the next. At one point I look to my right and see a sea of faces. I look down. It is easier for me not to see exactly how deep in I am.

Finally we have completed seven circuits and I almost cry with relief. This is my third *tawaaf*. This one has been made in the full crush of people. I feel I have achieved something. I also feel wonderfully at peace after my lengthy dialogue with God.

My cousin and I decide to meet again for *asr* prayers the next day, and to do another *tawaaf*. I also promise her that I will do a *tawaaf* on the upper floor with her, which will take twice as long because the circuit runs on the outside perimeter of the *mataff*, but it will be less stressful.

When I return to the hotel, rejuvenated, I learn from my roomies that they are planning to go by taxi to Jeddah the following day to visit family and to go shopping. I am invited to go along, but can't see myself traipsing around from shop to shop.

'I'll stay here and hold the fort,' I say.

Day 16 – Wednesday December 29th 2004

I have the room to myself and decide to work flat out on my laptop and to break only for prayers.

As I promised my cousin, I go to the Haram, to the spot where she said I should meet her for the afternoon prayers. We are going to pray together, and then go for a *tawaaf*. But she isn't where she said we should meet, and after prayers I come back to the hotel. I am not too concerned. The Haram is a big place. Perhaps she was looking for me elsewhere. It's easy to mistake one place for another. And tomorrow's another day.

Day 17 – Thursday December 30th 2004

10.00 a.m. I go down to the Haram to perform a *tawaaf*. I notice that the Kiswah – the black silk cloth covering the Kab'ah – has been rolled up, and is now showing a few feet of white cloth. It has been rolled up high enough that we can see several feet of the huge, dark brown stone structure underneath. I am told that the old Kiswah will be removed when the *hujaj* are in Mina and Arafah, and a new one put on. I don't know how this will be achieved because the Kab'ah is huge. Apparently a crane with a long arm will be on the *mataff* outside the Haram to lift it off and replace it. How, I can't imagine. It will have to be a crane with a very long arm to extend over the mosque into the courtyard to reach all the way over the Kab'ah. I can't see how they will get it onto the *mataff* itself.

For now, every day is almost the same, and will be like this for the next two and a half weeks until hajj begins. Except for outings with the group, our time is spent in prayer and contemplation, and making as many *tawaafs* as we can manage in a day. With Mecca filling up, it is harder to get a spot in the mosque at prayer time, and we are going a lot earlier. It also means that it is becoming practically impossible to do a *tawaaf* around the Kab'ah with all the thousands of pilgrims on the *mataff*. But you can perform *tawaaf* upstairs on the first level also, and on the roof, although it takes much longer as you have a much wider area to travel around.

In the evening, our group is invited by another South African group, staying at the Al-Maqaam, to come for a *thik'r* – a night of reciting and remembrance of God. A *thik'r* night always has the regular koeksisters and cakes afterwards, but I am too tired. The others go. I go to bed.

Day 18 – Friday December 31st 2004

I remember only late in the morning that it is the last day of the year. I send off some SMSes. Our morning is busy. It is Friday, *jum'ah* prayers. We want to be sure of a place in the mosque so we take our ablutions early, and reach the mosque almost an hour before prayer time. Already the mosque is full, and we are told by the *asgharis* to go upstairs.

The sermon is long, and in Arabic. We don't understand, but listen respectfully. Out of nowhere an Arab woman all in black with a baby on her hip, and her left arm exposed, appears. She is walking through the rows of seated women on the floor. As she nears, I see that it is a deformed arm and, instead of a hand, ends in something that resembles a flipper. She is holding out this deformed arm for everyone to see. I cannot believe it. Right in the mosque, she is begging. While we watch, another woman appears. She too is holding out her hand, asking for money. Then two males appear. They are in the women's section! One has no hand, the other no left arm. I realise why they're in the mosque. On Fridays, there is a sermon, and while everyone is listening to the Imam, who is in the men's section, they have the congregation's full attention for their begging. And people are giving to them. We've been told that we must give to beggars. But it is frowned upon to beg in a mosque, and there is a big sign outside the Haram which states not only that it is forbidden to take photographs, but also that it is not dignified to beg. What disturbs me about the scene is that while the woman with the baby is receiving lots of rials, she just snatches the notes from whoever gives them without so much as a glance or nod of thanks. It is almost as if they are her due. Later, I am told that some of these beggars – the ones with no hands – have had their hands amputated for stealing.

After lunch, I go with the others to look at a few things in the street. The honesty of the vendors is refreshing. On more than one occasion we make a mistake with the rials as the notes all look the same and you have to turn them over to distinguish a five from a ten or a twenty. At least twice, a shop owner hands us back money. They will bargain, but they won't take what does not belong to them. On another occasion we had already agreed on a price and the goods were in a bag, and a shop owner gave back five rials – simply because we'd bought so much. Bargaining is vociferous, though, but on the whole you get good deals and very good value for your money. The silk scarves I bought earlier would cost R80 each or more in the Cape. I paid nine rials each, which is about R15.

One of the other women in the group also saw an outfit she liked in a boutique at the Hilton Hotel, and wasn't sure she wanted to buy it. The owner of the shop insisted she take it home and try it on – there's no trying on of outfits in shops. The woman didn't want the responsibility of taking it home. The man insisted. In the end, he put it in a bag and pressed it on her and she brought it home and tried it on, and decided to buy it. The point is, there was no paperwork done. He didn't ask for a hotel name or number. He trusted her with a 200 rial outfit. He knew that she knew that her hajj would be no good if she ran off with it.

There's also generosity with food. Food is plentiful in Mecca, and cheap. No one starves. You can't give a beggar food: they want rials. We bought dhal and mutton curry at an Indian place, and got the naan

free. And portions are big. Chicken and chips consists of four pieces of chicken and way too many chips. One order is always enough for two.

The fact is, though, that we are getting tired of chicken. Chicken here is prepared a number of ways, but none of us wants to see fowl for a very long time when we get home.

On my way back up to the room I see the notice pasted up at the lift, reminding us of the one-day excursion to Jeddah the following morning at ten. I want to see the place where the Kiswah is made in Mecca, but have no enthusiasm for the rest of the day, which will be spent walking around the malls in Jeddah, shopping.

Day 19 – Saturday January 1st 2005

The buses leave at ten. There are about 50 of us. Our first stop is at the Museum in Mecca, where we can see all the earlier body parts (accessories) of the Kab'ah and other relics of interest.

We arrive at a huge building and enter into an open area where there are large pictures of the Kab'ah and the Grand Mosque on the walls, as well as many other photographs. In a glass case we see two silver covers for the Black Stone – Hajr Al-Aswad. The Black Stone is laid into the corner foundation of the Kab'ah. I had always thought the silver covering was part of the stone.

There are granite stones from the Prophet's time (pbuh); the old steps to the Kab'ah; the first *mim-*

bar, the cloth covering for the door; the heavy bolts which held the Kiswah in place on top of the Kab'ah; and many other items from the past. The visit is too short, and I am hardly able to take in everything.

Special mention must be made of the Kiswah. Before Islam, it is said that the first one who covered the Kab'ah was Tubba' – As'ad Al-Himyari – who was shown in a dream that he should cover it, and did

so with leather. Then he was shown that he should cover it with red-striped Yemeni cloth. After Tubba', it was covered by many people during Jahiliyah – the Age of Ignorance. Anybody who wanted to cover the Kab'ah could do so, with any kind of fabric. Thereafter it was covered with different kinds of covers, including thick cloth, thin cloth, fine cloth and cloth interwoven with gold thread. The covers would be placed one on top of the other until they became too heavy or worn out, and would be removed and shared out or buried. During the Age of Jahiliyah, the Quraysh used to cooperate in covering the Kab'ah, and would impose this duty upon the tribes as much as they could.

After Islam, before the conquest of Mecca, the Prophet Muhammad (pbuh) and his Companions were not allowed to cover the Kab'ah. When Mecca was conquered, the Prophet (pbuh) still did not change the cover until it was burned by a woman who wanted to perfume it with incense. Then he covered it with Yemeni cloth, and the Caliphs Abu Bak'r, Um'r and Uth'man covered it with Qibati, a thin white cloth from Egypt.

Over the centuries the Kab'ah was covered with many different cloths, including, at one time, red brocade on the day of At-Tarwiyah, with Qibati on the day when the new moon of Rajab was sighted and with white brocade on the 27th day of Ramadan. When it was found that the white brocade was being damaged during the days of hajj, a fourth white cover was made for the day of At-Tarwiyah. Then it was covered with a green cloth, and finally with a black cloth. From that day it has always been covered with a black cloth.

The first of the kings to cover the Kab'ah after the end of the 'Abbasid period was the king of Yemen in 659 AH. He continued to cover it for a number of years. In 751 AH the king of Egypt set up a *waqf* – an endowment – to cover the Kab'ah with an outer black cover once a year and the tomb of the Prophet Muhammad (pbuh) with a green cover once every five years. But the *waqf* was dissolved at the beginning of the thirteenth century AH, after which the cover was made at the government's expense. Turkey, including whoever came into power after the Ottomans, had the exclusive right to provide the inner cover of the Kab'ah.

During the Saudi period, King Faisal bin Abdul Aziz Aal Sa'ud issued orders in 1383 AH that a new factory be built to make the cover of the Kab'ah. The factory was completed fifteen years later in Mecca, and was equipped with automatic looms for making the fabric. However, the traditional handcrafts associated with making the cloth were retained because of their high artistic value.

Back at the museum, we see first-hand the slow process of producing the Kiswah. The man behind the looms, or the weaver, has a year to complete his job. He is currently working on the green, inner

cover of the Kab'ah. No foreigners are allowed to work in the factory where the Kiswah is produced: only Saudis.

The Kiswah is replaced every year. This is done while the pilgrims are in Arafah so that the Haram will be empty. When the pilgrims leave Mecca after hajj, at the end of January, a new Kiswah is started. The old Kiswah is cut up and pieces of it are given to the dignitaries who've had the honour of being invited to see the inside of the Kab'ah when it was being cleaned.

We leave the museum and head for Jeddah, where our first stop is the mosque at which we perform the midday prayers. After that we are treated to lunch and then it's time for the late afternoon prayers, at another mosque, built on stilts on the Red Sea. After our visit we go to a large picnic area where we can walk around and have ice cream or coffee. It's almost time for the sunset prayers when we get back into the bus. This is the part of the trip that everyone is waiting for, the shopping part.

We head for the Corniche Mall. It is a few minutes to six. We are told that we have time to shop until ten that night, when the buses will depart. What am I going to do for four and a half hours in a mall, I wonder? I have a sore throat, and have no desire to traipse around from shop to shop.

On the second floor of the mall we take ablution and then take out our prayer mats. It is not out of the ordinary to put down your mat in a quiet corner as everything closes the moment the *athan* sounds. We make *salaah* in front of a camera shop, combining the sunset prayers with the last prayers of the day. We are travelling, so we're allowed to do that. Shoppers loll around and wait. Even if you are busy with a transaction when the *athan* sounds, the shop owner will tell you that you have to come back when prayers are over.

For the first hour, I follow some of my fellow pilgrims around to a few shops. It's not as if they haven't walked Medina and Mecca flat already and spent thousands of rials: they just have to shop more. Everything on the shopping lists has been ticked off and they're now buying for themselves. Just in case they need an extra set of scatter cushions, here's another set, and so and so are always complaining about having no tablecloths, so there's two. To be sure, you get good prices in Jeddah, but you get deals in your own country also. And do you really need those two extra pairs of Italian shoes for the winter, or that Indian outfit with the pieces of chipped mirror – one in burgundy and one in green – that you'll probably never wear or at best only wear once? It's as if something's been unleashed in the South African pilgrim. At home they're too stingy to go to the movies on a Wednesday night or on weekends because it costs a few rand more, and here they're buying 200 rial shoes for Boeta Mietjie's daughter's grandchild who can't even count to ten, and a slew of engraved necklaces just in case someone has a baby and you need to bring a gift. I leave them and go to the chemist for something for my throat.

The pharmacist is an Arab and speaks ten words of English. My throat is sore, I tell him, making signs with my hands. He's impatient, and doesn't wait for me to finish.

'You cough?'

'No, I don't cough, but ...'

'You have pain?'

'No pain. I just ...'

'Fever?'

'No. My throat is raspy.'

He frowns. He doesn't understand, and turns away from me, reaching for a box on a shelf behind him. He hands it to me. I look at it. Orafor.

'I suck this or chew it?'

'What?'

'Do I suck this?' I stick out my tongue, 'or chew?'

'No, no. No chew.'

'How much?'

'Six rials.'

I hand him the money. He's already turned to the next customer. I'm a woman. I look conspicuous in his shop. I notice, incidentally, that where the shop owners are from Pakistan or other places, there is far more friendliness.

I leave the pharmacy, get a double scoop of Movenpick ice-cream, and sit on a bench and watch the passing parade. The nightmare is almost over. In two hours I can get on the bus and suck on my lozenge and sleep all the way to Mecca.

Day 20 – Sunday January 2nd 2005

I wake up from a deep and troubled sleep when the phone rings at 5.00 a.m. It's the hotel, waking us up for *faj'r* prayers. I turn over on my side. The airconditioning, the fetid air in the room and the second-hand smoke have all taken their toll on me. I have a full-blown sore

throat and flu. I am feeling too wretched to go to mosque, and decide to perform my prayers at home. It is pointless pushing yourself. You have to conserve your strength and energy for the days ahead when you will spend five days travelling between Mina, Arafah and Muzdalifah, with no sleep except for forty winks here and there.

I get up for the midday prayers and make it to mosque, but have no juice to go and make a *tawaaf*. The streets and the Haram are getting fuller, and it seems as if Mecca itself is hotting up. I have an early night. The others decide to make a *tawaaf* at eleven o'clock when the Haram is not so full.

Day 21 – Monday January 3rd 2005

I go for *faj'r* prayers at the mosque. The Haram is packed at 5.15 a.m. and the first thing I notice is that all the Persian mats have been removed. Later, when I go on my own to *tawaaf*, I notice the same thing throughout the mosque. They've been removed to create space for more people to pray. The mats create aisles between the rows. Without the mats, more people can be squeezed in.

After the afternoon prayers, I return to the hotel and spend the rest of the day indoors.

Day 22 – Tuesday January 4th 2005

I've developed a hacking cough. I go to mosque for *faj'r*, and straight after go for a *tawaaf*, which takes about 45 minutes. In the afternoon, my cough gets worse, and my body has the feeling of fatigue that comes with flu. I am not happy. I cannot afford to be sick for Mina and Arafah, when it's really going to be hectic. The two and a half weeks in Mecca have been arranged so that one can rest up and prepare oneself, not become weak.

I decide to change my routine and do my afternoon and evening prayers in the hotel room; and start a course of antibiotics, and rest.

Day 23 – Wednesday January 5th 2005

Feeling much better. Up at 5.00 a.m. I leave early for mosque, but cannot get within 30 feet of the entrance, and have to pray outside. It's a great morning – winter for the Arabs, but too hot for me at 30 degrees.

I have on a thin black robe with only a petticoat underneath. I have stopped wearing the long pants a week ago. It's amusing to see the Arabs come out with their jackets and blankets, the little children in winter clothes. It's the feeling of a change of season, I suppose, more than anything.

After prayers, I get ready to enter the mosque. I have two bags slung over my shoulder. The first is the big white cloth one with my prayer mat, my shoes in a plastic bag, two prayer books, tissues, a hand towel, and a handful of dates for afterwards, when I will take a drink of *zamzam* and watch the crowd below from the second floor balcony.

The second bag is a small, sandwich-size bright-red straw bag slung around my neck. This is the decoy bag, where I usually keep my digital Canon. But my camera isn't in there; I have removed it from its soft pouch within the red bag, and hidden it in my rolled-up prayer mat, which is in the white bag. A big bag like mine begs to be investigated by the *asgharis*, and I'm familiar by now with their methods of searching. They open the Velcro and feel inside at the bottom of the bag for cameras or guns. They've never searched my red bag, which I've always left empty and worn just as a test. This is the first time I am trying to take the camera into the Haram, hidden between the folds of my prayer mat. It is not my intention to take a picture inside. Not yet. I'll have to be extremely brave the day I make that move. They'll take the camera, or put me in jail, but I have it on me today so I don't have to go back to the hotel to fetch it. I want to go walking around afterwards to take shots.

Because I prayed outside on the *mataff*, no one searched my bag. But prayers have ended and it's time to go inside. The female *asgharis* are in full force outside the doors. I've thought about my reaction if they should discover the camera. No talking, no explanations. Just bolt! Disappear into the crowd. The women in their black robes are never going to catch me. Not unless they shout to alert the male *asgharis*. And then there'll be trouble.

A friend we met on the same floor had gone out with his camera

just the day before and taken a picture of some people standing in front of a small mosque. The flash had gone off and an Arab woman standing nearby had started to scream and push him around, accusing him of having taken her picture. A male *asghari* had come running and there had been a big commotion on the street. The *asghari* had taken the camera and ripped out the film. All our friend's other shots had been destroyed.

I move up to the entrance. Prayers have just ended, and there's a rush of people through the door. The *asgharis* have to look in all directions, but are more concerned with people coming in than with those leaving. I spot a gap between two of them and try to walk through. I am stopped. Two gloved hands reach into my white bag. I hold it out for inspection. She gropes around at the bottom, and then waves me along.

I go into the Haram, and edge my way very slowly through the crowd to the courtyard. I cannot believe how full it is. But I will try to do a *tawaaf*. I step down into the moving wheel of people. It's so overwhelming that even though I am on the perimeter of the crowd, within seconds I am swallowed up and trapped in the middle, with hundreds of faces around me. I cannot move. The crowd is at a complete standstill at the brown line where the *tawaaf* starts. I fight my way out sideways. It takes several minutes to extricate myself from the swell of bodies. I stand for a while on the top of the steps to catch my breath, then go for a drink of *zamzam*, and go upstairs to the next level where a *tawaaf* will take almost twice as long, but where you won't be jammed into another's back. This morning I saw a whole delegation of Chinese Muslims arrive to perform their *umrah* and *tawaaf*. Mecca is filling up.

I reach the second level and walk to the big green neon sign, which says, BEGINNING AND COMPLETION OF TAWAAF. This is where the brown line is, on which you place your right foot first before you raise your hands towards the Kab'ah, and say, *Bismillahi lilahita Allah, Allahu Akbar*, and start walking. When you have gone all the way around and come back to the same spot, you have completed one circuit. I do the first circuit for the sake of God, the second circuit for the holy Prophet Muhammad (pbuh), the third for my deceased parents, the fourth for my children, the fifth for my brothers and sisters, the sixth for my friends, and the seventh for myself.

The *tawaaf* leaves me feeling wonderfully refreshed after a day of holing up in the hotel. I decide to come back after lunch and do it again. It's not just a mindless walk. You are reciting silently all the time. You are having a brisk and invigorating walk. You are walking amongst people from all parts of the globe. There is movement, there is life, with something new to see at every turn. Even if you are uttering nothing except *Allahu Akbar* – God is Great – you are making *ibadah*. It is much like my walks at home – whether in Diep River, or on the Muizenberg beach, admiring the waves, the shells, the sand. Whenever you admire God's handiwork, you are doing something good.

In the end I do not take those forbidden photographs.

Day 24 – Thursday January 6th 2005

I am missing my son Faramarz and my helper Georgina and the dogs and my home, and am waiting anxiously for the days of Mina and Arafah and Muzdalifah to arrive. I have heard so much about how strenuous these five days are that I just want them to come. Mecca is a grind. It is constant. There's no letting up. I enjoy my time in the Haram, and take a lot of pleasure from a *tawaaf*, but your minutes and hours are all scheduled. Your activities, work and rest happen only between the *waq'ts*. There's no deviation. I can see now how absolutely lax I've been at home with my *salaah*. When I am in the comfort of my own home, I am always too busy and will procrastinate until the *waq't* is almost over. Now, I am jostled into action by the sound of the *athan*, drop what I am doing, take ablution and leave for the Haram right away. By the time you've performed *salaah* and walked home, 40 minutes have gone.

As I write this, it is taking longer to walk to and from the Haram with the rapidly swelling crowd. This morning I made it all the way into the Haram. This afternoon, I am praying on the steps in front of the Hilton Hotel.

Nevertheless, I have a different perspective and appreciation now. My prayers at home take only about ten minutes. If I have come to Mecca for no other reason than to appreciate how easy I've had it and how much easier it should be now upon my return, I've already learnt something. But then hajj is all about lessons. You only hope that when you get home, you remember.

In Mecca you see a lot of things. I have lived in the cosmopolitan

city of Toronto for 27 years, and have met and seen people from many different parts of the world, but have not encountered anything like this. I am seeing whole groups of people from other countries. They are dressed in particular colours, headdresses, robes, face coverings and pants with frilly or  embroidered cuffs to identify themselves. After a while, you see the beige dresses and white scarves, and you give way for the stocky Turks. You watch out for them in the Haram: they have good elbow action for knocking you out of the way. And they walk fast, even the women of 60 and over. I have seen very few young Turks; most of them are men and women in their late years. The Indonesians are a gentle people. And the Indians. It is heartbreaking sometimes to see people so anxious to be in this holy place, but so unworldly that they are afraid to step onto an escalator. Many of the old and indigent have been given the opportunity to come on hajj through government and other sponsorship.

And whole books can be filled with photographs just of the heels of the women in the Haram. Indian heels, African heels, European heels.

This afternoon, I prayed outside on the *mataff* and sat behind an African woman so black that I marvelled at the shine of her satiny feet, which reminded me of polished alabaster. Her heels, though, were so cracked that they looked as if someone had taken a hatchet and made splice marks all around them, with a road map of cuts on the sole of the foot, dark as clogged arteries. The most unbelievable feature of the foot, however, was that the top was a black hue tinged with claret. In between her toes the skin was blackberry red. Around the bottom edge of the foot was a dark line – as if her foot had soaked for hours in a shallow bed of black mud.

I touched her on the leg. She turned. I pointed to her feet.

'Henna?'

She smiled. An exquisite face. Delicate features.

'What country?' I ask.

She looks confused. I point to myself. 'Sud Afrika.'

She nods that she understands. 'Mali.'

I have never met anyone from Mali. And I have seen thousands of hennaed feet now in my few weeks in the country, but this is truly a work of art. And she's so delicate and fine that I am thinking of asking her if I can photograph her feet afterwards, but I can't make myself understood without taking out the camera – hidden in an inner pocket now – and there wouldn't be five inches of space anywhere nearby where I could do it. I leave there, after prayers, with nothing.

I've had enough warnings about cameras and *asgharis*. I have also been told by some people not to come back and talk about the bad things in Mecca. I've always wondered what those bad things might be. Would I see things that would take away from the spirit of the holy city

and contaminate my view of it? I wasn't so naïve as to believe that just because Mecca is known as the Sacred City and the place where Muslims come together in pilgrimage, I would find it pristine, especially as I've also heard many times that 'the devil is loose in Mecca, keep your faith'. The devil business is a myth. It's not the devil, but people's true behaviour surfacing. People get to know one another quite well when they're crammed together into a limited space for an extended period of time. They see quirks and behaviours and idiosyncrasies they've never seen before. Is it the devil when a woman goes to Mecca and comes back with someone else's husband? Did the devil make her do it? Or is it just lack of control?

Mecca, from before the Prophet's time (pbuh), has always been a place of trade, and still is today. Tall elegant buildings keep company with the old and dilapidated. Alleyways, bazaars, people eating on the streets, buses, construction sites, cars and their incessant hooters. Always there is something to sell, and always there is someone who is willing to pay for it. Even a beggar, when he pleads for money, is selling his condition – counting on your sympathy to give him a few rials.

But what are the bad things I shouldn't talk about? In any place where you're going to have millions of people converging on a particular area for any length of time, you're bound to have chaos, unless your preparation for the event is superb. Millions of people have to eat, they have to sleep, they have to relieve themselves. Before, pilgrims could come for hajj without having procured hotel accommodation. This resulted in pilgrims from the poorer countries sleeping in tunnels and under bridges, and creating unsanitary conditions. Not so any more. You can't enter Mecca unless you have lodgings. The city has been cleaned up. The Saudis are spending millions. But of course,

you're going to have litter. And a week ago, someone spat right on my foot in the street. I had to wipe it off with a tissue, and rush off to the hotel to wash.

The clean-up procedures in Mecca are swift, and something to marvel at. With thousands of pilgrims and traders clogging the streets, you have motorised vehicles with electric brooms going up and down daily to suck up the dirt. At the Haram, you'll see seven or eight men with long brooms and buckets of water washing down the marble *mataff*. Even with the multitudes performing *tawaaf* around the Kab'ah, you'll see the clean-up squad cordon off a section, move the

people to one side, clean and polish the *mataff*, before cordoning off the next section. When the mats were still down inside the mosque, the carpet cleaners did the same thing. The Haram and the streets are cleaned daily.

Mecca is old. It is holy. It is cosmopolitan. It is busy. But on the mountain a few kilometres away, where the holy Prophet Muhammad (pbuh) received his first revelation, everything is still as it was fourteen hundred years ago.

There is nothing bad to report. It is a city steeped in the past.

9.30 p.m. We go downstairs to the mezzanine floor. The group is having a *thik'r* – reciting – and also celebrating the birthday of the Imam's son. Afterwards, there will be a motivational talk about the forthcoming hajj.

We are fifteen minutes late, and arrive to a room full of people. The men are seated on the floor on blankets, the women on chairs. On one side of the room, a table groans under platters of cakes and desserts and nuts and chips and chocolates and drinks. The *thik'r* has started: we sit down and join in reciting.

After the *thik'r* is over an hour later, Imam Abdullah talks about preparing and building up for the days of Arafah.

'People, in five days we're going to be there. It's not going to be easy. You're not going to be sleeping on Posturepedics, and under thick blankets. You're going to be in a tent, you'll be sleeping on a mat. You can buy a mattress: they'll be selling them there. And don't bring blankets. If it's the *taqdir* of Allah that you must get cold, you'll get cold. Also, the Saudis will provide the food. In Cape Town, when they say breakfast is at seven, it's at seven. On Arafah and Mina, if they say it's at eight, it might come at two in the afternoon. Just have *sab'r*. There'll be millions of people on Arafah, they have to see to everyone. This isn't going to be five-star treatment, but *inscha Allah*, we'll have a five-star hajj.'

Day 25 – Friday January 7th 2005

7.00 a.m. A *tawaaf* on the roof of the Haram. I am by myself. Even though the distance around the Kab'ah is longer up here, I can walk faster, and it only takes seven minutes to do a circuit. The morning is cool. There are only a few hundred pilgrims on the roof. It's a beautiful start to my day. I have such a dialogue with God that I feel cleansed.

Jum'ah prayers, however, almost turn into a nightmare. It is our third Friday in Mecca. Day by day the streets are becoming more congested. When I step down from the hotel steps onto the street, I am immediately part of thousands of *hujaj* inching their way up the street to the Haram. I get to the mosque an hour before prayer time. I am turned away by the *asgharis* at three entrances. I get to the fourth, and make it to the second level, but the place is so full that there isn't space between any of the rows of women seated on the floor for me to throw down my prayer mat. I walk between the rows. I cannot believe that the mosque can be so jammed tight with people an hour ahead of prayers.

I see a space of about four or five inches between two women, and go over to them. They are Turkish women in beige outfits and white scarves. I indicate with my hand that I want to sit between them, and ask whether they can shift up a bit. One of the women waves her hand at me, and tells me to shove off, pointing to indicate that I should go to the front of the mosque to look for a place. I am taken aback by her attitude: you're supposed to make place for someone. I see two other women further on; I might be able to squeeze my mat in between them. One of these women is Arab and is even ruder. When I refuse to move, she hits me with her bare hand on my foot. A woman with thick legs sitting a few feet away watches all this. She is a big woman, with not a hand's width between herself and the Indian woman next to her. She waves to me to come. I am grateful, and take my mat over. I fold my *muslah* in half – there is no space to spread it out in full – and fit in between her and the other woman. I sit propped up between them for almost an hour before prayers start.

As I am sitting there, I look at her feet. How does this woman walk, I wonder? She has a bunion on her right foot the size of a boiled egg. The Indian woman's feet have 'village' written all over them. I smile at both of them, thanking them.

I hear a crackling of voices up ahead. I look up and see several women bent over someone, waving their hands vociferously, trying to circulate the air. A woman has fainted from the heat. She recovers after some time. I wipe my own brow. *Please, God, give me strength for the rest of this journey.*

When prayers are over, the nightmare of leaving the mosque and getting to the hotel begins. There have to be over a million people in the mosque and its precincts, all of them trying to get out so that they can go in their different directions. The worst part is on the *mataff* near the exit where thousands of people create a bottleneck trying to get onto the road. I am jammed between young and old, men and women, bad breath, sweaty bodies, as they push and shove from all

sides. I simply can't move. Someone steps on the back of my shoe and it almost comes off. A huge man behind me has his elbow in my back. Another, an Afghan by the look of his turban, is praying in a loud voice on my left, beseeching God that he not be crushed. I can't take it, but I can't afford to panic either. After five or ten minutes, there is sudden relief as we step onto the road and have a few inches of breathing space. What am I going to do at *asr* prayers, I ask myself? The situation has clearly worsened. A four-minute walk to the Haram now takes twenty minutes. It's not the time: it's the jostling, the fear of being trampled on. If a shoe comes off, there's no stopping. You step over many lost shoes.

Asr arrives. We get to the hotel steps. We realise immediately that we will never make it to the Haram in time. We walk five paces from the hotel, and throw down our mats in front of a shop. For the evening prayers, we do the same thing.

Day 26 – Saturday January 8th 2005

An introspective kind of day. I withdraw. Do a lot of reading. Perform prayers on the street outside the hotel. Not in the mood for chitchat.

In today's *Arab News*, it states that Saudi Arabia has issued over 1,2 million visas for pilgrims intending to perform hajj, and that *umrah* visas issued during the current year increased by 16 per cent to more than 2,6 million, with the largest number arriving during Ramadan. Around 7 500 hajj visas have been granted to South Africans.

The need for hajj visas relates to health conditions: pilgrims must show that they have received the required vaccinations to ensure their safety as well as the safety of other pilgrims.

The paper also reports that Saudi Arabia has offered SR339 000 to finance the hajj arrangements for 39 relatives of 13 Indians who died in the stampede during the last annual pilgrimage. The pelting of the Jamarah in Mina is what we're all a little apprehensive about. Not only will there be multitudes of people there, but they will be spiritually charged, making for a frenzied atmosphere.

In the evening I call my son. Everything is all right at home. Georgina is looking after things nicely. The dogs are fine.

Day 27 – Sunday January 9th 2005

Three hours on the roof by myself. I do a *tawaaf*, go to the bookstore at the Hilton to buy a book and come back to the Haram, where I sit on the roof reading, a cup of *zamzam* and a handful of dates at my side. I love dates. I have bought five different varieties to bring home. They give you complex carbohydrates and sugars, and lots of fibre. A piece of cheese and an apple, with a few hardy dates, will suffice for lunch.

Today, in *The Saudi Gazette*, it is stated that the Saudis have put together a comprehensive plan to provide all possible facilities to more than two million visitors to the Prophet's Mosque in Medina and the Grand Mosque in Mecca.

'For the Grand Mosque in Mecca, in addition to some 800 regular staff, over 2 000 will be appointed temporarily for the season to provide extra services to pilgrims.

'A labour force of 3 500 will be on duty around the clock for cleaning the inside and open plazas. They will use auto-cleaning machines. The labour force is divided into teams: to clean the toilets, bathrooms and ablution places. They will use disinfectants to stop the spread of germs and viruses. Other teams will spread the prayer carpets of 3 x 4 metres covering an area of more than 100 000 metres in the open plazas and inside the Holy Mosque.

'Another team will supply *zamzam* water to more than 15 000 thermoses. They are assigned to clean them and provide new plastic glasses and remove the used ones. The team consisting of the technicians and electricians attached to the Holy Mosque is responsible for maintaining all electricity connections and appliances. They look after the cameras fitted in and around the mosque. Another team will look after the nine escalators.

'Another section supplies more than 10 000 wheelchairs to the handicapped pilgrims free of cost. The security and peace force will be on duty at all 70 gates of the mosque. They will also be on watch and ward duty to act against anyone breaching the peace. They will keep a strict watch for thieves and pickpockets on the *mataff*.

'The Prophet's Mosque in Medina, which accommodates a million worshippers, has also been provided with all first grade facilities and comforts for the visitors.

'The regular staff, along with the watch and ward staff numbering 1 777, have been appointed for offering general services, guidance, assistance to the disabled and supervision of all labour. A labour force of about 3 000 workers usually carries out cleaning of the mosque by auto-cleaners, lifting of the carpets for cleaning the ground, and again spreading them in the entire mosque and in its open courtyards on all four sides of the mosque.

'The Presidency has engaged twenty big water tankers to supply 200 tons of *zamzam* water from Mecca on a daily basis to the Prophet's Mosque. Water is cooled at 23 big plants and later used to fill 7 000 thermoses for visitors.

In the evening at the mosque, the Imam announces that there will be special prayers for rain in Mecca the following morning at 7.00 a.m.

Day 28 – Monday January 10th 2005

I go to the Haram by myself. I do a *tawaaf* and then sit in the mosque and read. I leave before the masses arrive for the midday prayers. I do this because while I am already in the mosque and will have no problem getting a spot, it will take me an hour or more to get out when prayers are over. I have decided that I will spend two or more hours a morning in the mosque so that I won't feel bad when I have to do the rest of my prayers in the street.

After eighteen days in Mecca I can understand why my cousin Farooq, who came on hajj last year, did not mind leaving Mecca to go to Azizia for the last two weeks before hajj. This is encouraged to facilitate the influx of pilgrims in the later weeks when accommodation around the Haram is more expensive – and your package, going through to

Azizia, can be a little less costly. But a lot of *hujaj* opt not to go to Azizia because of the hassle of moving again, and the inconvenience of having to take either a taxi or shuttle service into Mecca every day.

According to my cousin, however, it's a relief and a bit of a break to go to Azizia as you've had the pleasure of being in Mecca while it was less crowded, and can now let other people have a chance. Also, he says, being in Mecca is hard. You spend all your time trying to get in and out of the Haram for prayers. You go an hour before the time, and you are hardly out before it is time to go again. In Azizia, there are many mosques, and there's always place; you don't have to go before the time. Also, it gives you a bit of a rest before hajj starts.

This morning, battling my way up the short road to the Haram an hour after prayers are over, I remember his words. He was indeed right. It is virtually impossible to get into the mosque unless you go an hour and a half before the time. And you can forget about a *tawaaf* around the Kab'ah now. You have to go after midnight, or go to the first level, or the roof. I stand with my mat anywhere I can find a spot in the street. As long as you are following the Imam in prayer, it carries the same weight as if you are in the Haram.

In the evening, just a day after finishing a course of antibiotics, I feel a sore throat starting up again. I take a lozenge and go to bed. I am going to try my best not to take antibiotics again. However, Arafah is looming. I can't afford to be weak.

Day 29 – Tuesday January 11th 2005

Wake up with a wretched throat and decide to take it easy and do all my prayers in the hotel. The imams will look for the moon tonight. If they sight the moon, we are leaving for Mina next Wednesday. If not, our departure will be on the Thursday.

Day 30 – Wednesday January 12th 2005

They've sighted the moon! We will leave for Mina next Wednesday. I still have a wretched throat and have contracted full-blown flu now. I am considering antibiotics again, but will wait another day to see whether there's any improvement. I have to be hardy and fit for next week's travels. Yesterday we were again warned that we had to prepare ourselves for the hardships ahead.

'Prepare yourself for a problem. Take your own water. Drinking water, and water to clean yourself. And don't forget your torch if you want to go to the toilet at night.'

Terrible heat in the room. Stuffy and fetid. Airconditioning blasting cold air and redistributing dust in the room. I lose my voice within minutes. To add to the discomfort, children ranging from three to twelve are running up and down in the passage until after 3.00 a.m., keeping us from sleep.

Day 31 – Thursday January 13th 2005

I have not been outside for two days, and am told that the vendors and traders have been cleared off the streets to make room for pilgrims. It is now so full that the members of our group are praying in the foyer of the hotel.

I am still sick. My body feels heavy with flu. One of my roommates has a full packet of antibiotics and offers them to me. I am hesitant. I don't know what they are, and don't know what constitutes a full course. Still, I am feeling bad enough that I do take them. In the lift, I see one of the owners of the Royal Group – he lives on our floor – and ask whether he might be able to help me get to SAHUC as I need a doctor. He says he will arrange for someone to take me. SAHUC has a

South African doctor on call and you get properly diagnosed and don't pay anything for medication. You have paid for this already as part of your package.

Six hours later, I am still waiting. I see the owner's wife in the kitchen and ask her to remind him. Medication can be a real problem for pilgrims in Mecca, with people for the most part diagnosing themselves. We are all told to bring antibiotics with us, and so we come with a broad spectrum antibiotic, and at the first sign of a sniffle, take a pill. We feel better the next day and stop taking the pills; but antibiotics have to be taken as a full course. For my first really bad setback with a sore throat the previous week, I had taken a full course of the antibiotics I had brought with me. One day after completing the course, I got a sore throat again. It could be that the antibiotic wasn't strong enough, or that I was fighting a losing battle against the claustrophobic conditions and airconditioning in the room. With a million people on the street, Mecca is rife with germs and many people wear protective, face-hugging white masks. Some get lucky and never get a cold. Even though I had a flu injection before leaving home, I am not so lucky.

Day 32 – Friday January 14th 2005

Five days to Mina. Time is drawing near. We are both apprehensive and excited. On Sunday night we will have a lecture to prepare us further for the five days ahead.

I am still on my roommate's medication, and feeling a bit better. Taking every precaution to ensure that I stay healthy.

It is *jum'ah* today. You now have to go to the Haram at 10.00 a.m. to secure a spot for the 12.30 p.m. prayers. We have given up and have decided that for the rest of our stay in Mecca we will pray with the rest of the group in the lobby of the hotel. When we reach downstairs, however, it is already full, with the hotel door locked so outsiders can't come in. It is pleasant, though, to pray downstairs in the lobby, and a far cry from throwing your mat on the street.

With the crowds, however, it is also difficult to go out after prayers to buy food. As much as possible, we try to make our own, otherwise one of the men goes out and buys food for everyone with the money in the kitty. The food is always tasty, and we have had some superb channa dhal, but

I must be honest and say that I miss my salmon and crackerbread, and would like to get back to my normal way of eating. The only thing I wish we had in Cape Town was the great variety of dates.

Day 33 – Saturday January 15th 2005

Quiet day. Eat, sleep, prayers in the lobby. I am well enough to go out with the others for a midnight *tawaaf*.

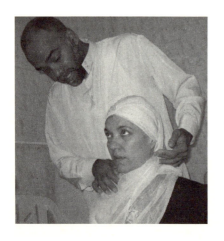

Day 34 – Sunday January 16th 2005

This morning, when I get up, Rashad – the guy who shares a room with the men in our group – is busy pinning the medorahs of two women in the kitchen. A medorah is a square chiffon-type scarf with gold or silver threading. It's an art to pin a medorah – usually worn by a *hujaj* when arriving from Mecca, or by a bride or bridesmaids.

Wherever you look, the women are busy preparing their outfits and headgear for when they go home. We will all travel by bus to Jeddah, take a flight to Cairo, change to a flight for Johannesburg, then board a last flight to Cape Town. Medorahs and outfits will be carefully packaged for the *hujaj* to change into at Johannesburg International Airport. I remember my brother Shaheen telling me that when he returned from Mecca, he came home in the same clothes in which he had made his last *tawaaf*.

I have nothing elaborate planned, but had packed a plain white robe with a high collar and a black *abayah*. The outfit had been a gift which had come with a wedding proposal from an Egyptian, Muhammad, while I was living in Canada years ago. I accepted the gift, but married the Egyptian's Egyptian friend, whose name was also Muhammad. Alas, the *abayah* has survived both Muhammads, who both remain good friends.

Today, *Arab News* reports that the Kingdom has made adequate security arrangements to secure the safety of pilgrims during the coming hajj.

'Police reinforcements have been deployed at the entrances to Mecca and on the roads leading to the holy sites in order to facilitate traffic. Over 14 200 buses will be used to transport pilgrims within the holy sites. More than 50 000 security men have been deployed to secure hajj. Between 70 and 80 per cent of their task is primarily concerned with traffic control and ensuring the safety of pilgrims. More than 10 000 officers have been deployed to deal with any developments related to security matters.

'Yesterday security was tight throughout the holy sites of Mina, Muzdalifah and Arafah to prevent stampedes or other incidents or accidents. At checkpoints several kilometres outside Mecca, security personnel were seen stopping cars randomly, peeking into trunks, shining mirrors to look for explosives in undercarriages and checking IDs and other personal documents. A fleet of 3 000 vehicles, 10 000 officers and 15 aircraft have been pressed into service to make hajj smooth and incident-free.

'The Kingdom is taking extra safety measures to avoid the kind of stampede during the ritual of stoning that over the past years has claimed many lives. Also, special emphasis will be given to the safety of pilgrims in the sprawling tent city of Mina.

'Mina looked all bedecked to receive its annual visitors. The cleaning and maintenance of tents, roads and drinking points, as well as installation of safety equipment, have been completed. The Ministry of Health has also completed its preparation for the protection of pilgrims from any outbreak of diseases. They are also watching for any signs of epidemics, particularly among pilgrims from tsunami-hit areas. Thus far, none has been spotted.'

I don't think I can explain to the reader how massive this operation is. Mecca is on full alert. Pilgrims of all description – young, old, very old, black, white and brown – have all converged on Mecca to make the journey of a lifetime, to perform the rituals of hajj, which climaxes on Wednesday with the 'standing' on Mount Arafah. With nearly three million Muslims from all over the world gathering in a geographic capsule in preparation for their religious duty, Mecca has turned into a sea of seamless white clothes.

11.00 p.m. Pilgrims congregate downstairs for a final meeting before departure for Mina on Tuesday. Imam Abdullah Adams gives us the hard facts. Two buses have been contracted to pick us up at 7.00 on Tuesday morning to take us to the tent city of Mina. If the buses are not here by 8.00 or 9.00, we are not to panic. Under ordinary circumstances, every one has a seat. For hajj, there will be a hundred people per bus. The women will be *in* the bus, the men will be on top. And the women who will get a seat will be the ones who get on the bus first.

He talks about our stay at Muzdalifah and how easy it will be to get lost. We are to take the cell numbers of the group leaders. In the event that we do get lost, we know the procedure. We have to have money on us for a taxi to take us back to Mecca. There will be no taxis in Mina, but there will be a few, after pelting, in Muzdalifah. He relates a story of a husband and wife a few years ago who had  been together the whole time. And then, when the time came to board the bus, one stood in front of the bus, and the other stood on the other side. Owing to the crowds, one never got onto the bus and they didn't see each other again for two days.

'I also want to talk about the food. You will be fed for the five days. Because of the fire disaster a few years ago, the food will be made on the outskirts of Mina and brought in. Now, if the food doesn't have a lot of onions in it, like we're used to in Cape Town, that's just how it is. And if you get breakfast in the afternoon, there's nothing we can do. Have your biscuits and your dates. Bring fruit. And I want to talk also about having consideration for one another tomorrow when you're taking your *ghus'l* to go into *ihram*. Having water in Mecca isn't like having water in Cape Town, where we have the Steenbras dam. Here, you see the water trucks come every day to give the hotel water. When all the traffic is going one way on the days of Mina, and no one is allowed to go the other way, the water trucks also won't be allowed in, and there won't be water. So don't stand under the shower and waste time. Use the water sparingly, and get out. And don't send little children by themselves into the shower. Have an adult go in and wash them. If we don't do this, there won't be water for everyone.'

The meeting concludes at half past one in the morning.

Day 35 – Monday January 17th 2005

I go down for the midday prayers to the hotel lobby. When the elevator reaches the ground floor, there is no room to step out. Men are praying right up against the bank of elevators. I go back up to perform *salaah* in my room.

We will spend a quiet day in preparation for departure tomorrow morning at dawn. We will take our turns in the shower, saying a special *niyyah* to go back into *ihram* to go to Mina. Two buses have been contracted to take us. The people I came with will do a walking hajj. I will go with them. We will not get on the bus, which will probably take three or four hours with the traffic, to drive nine kilometres. Each one will carry their own provisions for the next two days, after which we return to Mecca to perform an *ifaldah tawaaf* and a *saee*, and then return to Mina for two more days.

In today's *Arab News*, it is reported that 112 pilgrims have died in Medina before performing hajj. Most died of natural causes, with five pilgrims dying as a result of accidents. A Dutch woman and a Thai man died as a result of traffic accidents; an Afghani and a Turk died when they fell from tall buildings; and an Indian pilgrim died of a fall in Mecca. All but one of the pilgrims was buried in Medina, the exception being a Pakistani whose body was returned to his country in accordance with his family's wishes.

In another section of the paper, under 'Islam demands purity of soul, body, mind & dress', there is some good advice for the five days of hajj.

'When pilgrims from around the world come to Mecca, what they find is usually beyond their anticipation or imagination. One of the unexpected occurrences is the huge assembly of pilgrims, all gathered in one area, performing the same rituals, facing the same direction, and dressed in simple white clothing. With such a large population in such a confined space under less than perfect conditions, it is impossible to avoid either the fact or the possibility of communicable diseases and illnesses.'

The article goes on to talk about vaccines and personal hygiene, and to pay particular attention to food.

'To remove parasites and undesirable microorganisms, raw fruits and vegetables should be treated in a special way. All greens, root vegetables and fruits, as well as other edible raw plants, should be soaked for 15 minutes in water with apple cider vinegar added to it.'

Hajj

Day 36 – Tuesday January 18th 2005

4.00 a.m. Waiting in lobby of hotel for the rest of the 'walking' hajj group to come down from their rooms. We are ready. We will not be taking the bus to Mina with the others. We will walk the eight or nine kilometres to the South African camp on the plains of Mina, and not have the frustration of sitting in a bus for three or four hours in the heat and traffic. Our bags are on our shoulders and backs. We have drinking water in bottles. My laptop is safely tucked away in the hotel safe; the next five days will all be recorded in handwritten notes. This now is the beginning of my hajj rituals. I am sick with a bad chest and flu, but can't think of that now.

4.40 a.m. We are joined by Sheikh Gabriels and his wife and six children. There are about 30 of us who are walking to Mina. First, however, we have to go to the Haram. We perform the *tahajud* prayers, which take place an hour before the *faj'r* prayers. There are thousands of pilgrims on the *mataff*. They are all waiting for the *athan*. It is apparent that they will all be walking as well.

5.45 a.m. We are finished with prayers. We start walking. We are headed, along with thousands of other pilgrims, towards the pedestrian tunnel. It leads uphill and cuts through one of the mountains of Mecca. Powerful airconditioning units overhead sound like the roar from the underbelly of a plane. Already I am cursing all the things in my overnight bag, which has a wide strap slung over my right shoulder. In my bag I have a packet of biscuits, a half-kilo of dates, a half-kilo of almonds, an apple, a Toblerone chocolate, tissues, toilet paper, vitamins, toothbrush and toothpaste, a hand towel, an extra pair of panties, my journal in which I am writing all of this, my reading glasses, my sunglasses, my prayer books. Around my neck hangs another purse, with my camera. I am wearing one jersey over my robe, even though it is hot already for this time of the morning, and have a shawl wrapped around my waist, so that I can cover myself at night in the tent. In my left hand I am carrying a bottle of drinking water and a spray bottle containing water, in the event that I have to perform ablution along the way.

One of the men is walking in front, carrying the South African flag. We are not to lose sight of this flag in the thick crowd. We are to keep together so as not to get lost.

I am walking with the men up front. My one-hour walks in the mornings at home, five times a week, are standing me in good stead. Still, I am carrying a load, my shoulder is hurting from the strap, and it's mostly uphill.

An hour later we emerge from the tunnel to a long strip of buildings and restaurants, built right into the mountainside. The roads are

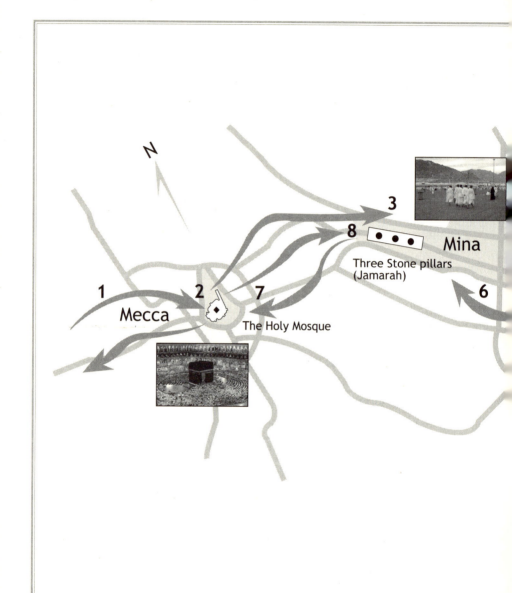

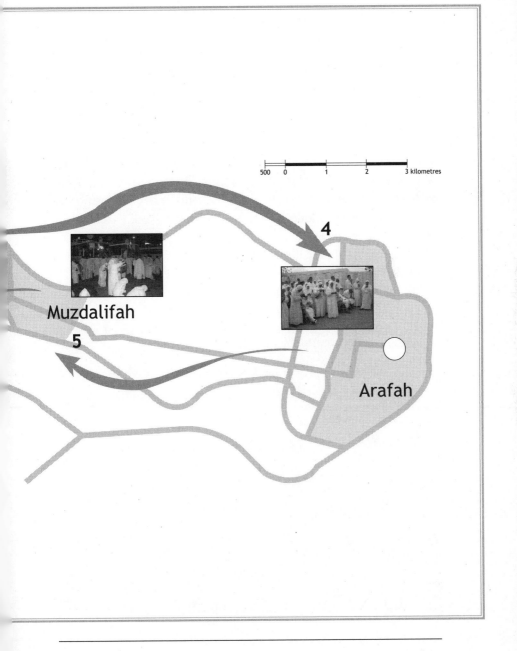

wide here, double carriageways with a grass median. The lanes on the other side of the median are filled with traffic. The pedestrian road we're on is a one-way: during hajj many roads are blocked off and there is traffic only in one direction for people doing the walking hajj into Mina. Those coming in buses will not be brought all the way to the camp, though. The buses will drop them off an hour from where they have to be.

I have to go to the toilet, but am hesitant to ask the group to stop. After another fifteen minutes the sheikh brings the group to a halt and says we're taking a break for fifteen minutes. But there's nowhere I can go. Restaurants here are not like the restaurants at home. Mostly you order your food at a window and take it along with you. There are no sit-down places along this strip, and no inside toilets – not even in Mecca, except for the big hotels like the Hilton and Sheraton. So I have to hold on.

We continue our walk. We have another hour or so to go. I can't believe that I have burdened myself with such a lot of things to carry when I could've bought water, juice and fruit along the way. I needn't have brought anything to eat. We are in a long straight tunnel now, with overhead lighting, stalls on the side, and thousands upon thou-

sands of pilgrims in tents and on blankets and sheets of cardboard and mats on the edges of the road. They are camped out for the five days. These are the pilgrims without groups and without accommodation, who will squat in Mina for the entire period of hajj. They take up a lot of space and narrow the road down considerably, making it difficult for ambulances and security personnel on motorbikes – the only vehicles allowed – to come through. The litter is unbelievable: juice boxes, milk cartons, Styrofoam containers, plastic bags, empty chip packets, candy wrappers, papers and plastics and sloffies, and empty boxes. The stench of sweat and dust and drain water and public toilet facilities hits your nostrils, and you wish you had put on your mask: masks are sold everywhere for one rial each.

But mostly, you are stunned by the crowd, amazed that there are people who would throw themselves down along the side of this dank road and stomach the thousands milling by, people stepping over and around them, trampling on the edges of their mats. A row of toilets for women is up ahead. I know that even though I need to go desperately, I will not attempt this knee-bending toilet five feet away from people milling on the street. After another half an hour, I tell the man with the flag that he has to stop. Someone comes with me and guards the door of the toilet I am in. I am in *ihram*: my white robe, white long pants, and long white petticoat. I put my Nike-shod feet gingerly on either

side of the porcelain hole in the ground. It is wet and slippery and stinks like last year's rotten cabbage water. But I can't do anything about it. I have to go. I roll up the bottoms of my pants, lift up my petticoat and dress and pull down the pants, while holding them carefully by their elastic waistband as I lower myself. It is at moments like these that you truly know who you are.

The walk continues. We have passed the campsites of many other countries already, and are heading for campsite 87. At last we come to the place where we have to turn left. The streets are all numbered and the flags are flying overhead. The streets teem with pilgrims. We don't know which way to go. One of the men decides to go on ahead to investigate, while about twenty of us park ourselves right on a median in the middle of the road and start to eat. After half an hour of waiting he comes back, and we follow him down the street, where we turn in at the section called Non-Arab African Nations (Zimbabwe, Nigeria, South Africa). We see the flag, and then the name of our tour group, Royal International, on two of the tents: one for the women and one for the men. We can't believe that after almost four hours of walking, we have arrived, at just after 10.00 a.m.

We go inside. The tent is huge, with central airconditioning, lights, proper ventilation and mats strewn over the whole area. There are some women there already, with their prayer mats thrown down at the spots where they will sit and sleep and eat for two days. Their shoes and bags are right next to them. Once all the women are in, there are about 50 of us. The men's tent is attached to ours. A slit in the canvas allows us to communicate.

Outside the tents, men and women are queuing in different lines for the toilets and ablution facilities. The site teems with people. It is the South African camp, meaning that all the various South African groups will be united in this section of the greater camp.

I take up my position at the end of the line for the toilets. I am tired from not having slept the previous night, and a little disoriented. We arrive early enough that I am able to choose a quiet corner, put down my things, spread out my prayer mat, and lay my weary body down on the hard ground, with my head on my overnight bag. I fall instantly asleep, and am woken up an hour later when the rest of the Royal Group arrives.

Lunch arrives just a little after the midday prayers: chicken curry with rolls, bottled water and Pepsi.

After lunch I go out. All the action takes place outside the tents, where people collect in groups and talk. I run into my cousin Mareldia, who is with another group. She has been very ill since the last time I saw her a few weeks ago in Mecca, and looks dreadful. Her sister-in-law, Garaatie, was also ill and had to be taken to hospital in an ambulance with an asthma attack. But they're both optimistic, taking their medication, and bracing themselves for the days ahead.

Once again we are lined up to go into a bank of toilets. There are seven in a row: the first one on the left, a regular toilet, is for women; the next two are for men or women and are the flat toilets. The next three are for men only, and the last one for women only – all flat toilets. The line for the regular toilet for women on the left is the longest, and at first I stand in this queue. It's not bad standing in a queue – unless you have a pressing need to go right away – as you get to talk to people, and can catch up with events and other people's experiences. I learn from my cousin that after she last saw me, she and her brother and her brother's wife had been moved to the second floor of their hotel, and then again to another floor. She was very unhappy with the group she'd travelled with, and had given up on ever receiving a refund for the mix-up with the rooms.

Half an hour later, I am still standing in the queue. I decide not to wait for the regular toilet any more, and go into one of the flat toilets. The shower is dripping overhead, directly over the toilet, and I have to squat, hold up my clothes, and hold my head and shoulders one side to avoid getting wet. I am not very successful and end up with a wet head. Still, with all the indignities of the toilet and inconvenience of living in a tent with 50 other women, I am glad to be out of the hotel room for a few days. Here there are new faces, fresh conversations and different ideas, with everyone forced to consider his or her neighbour, who is just inches away.

For supper we have mince curry. The food is tasty, and we are not disappointed. After supper, the men start to *thik'r*.

Imagine this huge tent with 50 women, the lights dimmed, the night winding down. The women are getting ready to sleep. We hear the men's voices, starting to rise,

Allah hu ...
Allah hu ...
Allah hu ...

Imam Abdullah is leading, reciting the main verse. The men come in with *Allah hu, Allah hu, Allah hu.*

The chanting is powerful. I am lying in the corner of the tent, facing the canvas. My world is a small one. I am alone, uttering *Allah hu*, quietly under my breath. My rhythm picks up, the tears flowing down my face. This is the state of all human beings, I think as I am lying there. We are alone. We come alone and will go alone, and in between we have to live.

I am crying, wiping my face with my hands in the half-light. *Here I am, God. You summoned me. You created me. Here I am.*

It was the first time that I had placed myself completely in God's hands.

Day 37 – Wednesday January 19th 2005

3.00 a.m. I am standing in a long queue, waiting to go to the toilet and take ablution. Our day is starting very early.

4.00 a.m. The buses arrive and we leave for Arafah. This is the big day. This is the day we will *wuqoof* – spend the whole day in prayer and remembrance of God, and beg God to forgive us for all our sins. *Wuqoof* is hajj.

The ride is a short one, and we arrive half an hour later at a tent in darkness: there is no light. In this tent the men and women will be together – the men on the far side, the women on the right. One or two women have torches, and we are able to secure a spot for ourselves and throw down our mats. We perform *faj'r* prayers. Shortly after, an announcement is made that we are to queue outside for blankets. We are eager for something to cushion our backs on the hard ground, and line up. We are also given a toiletry pack with toothbrush and paste, soap, and a few facemasks.

The tents here are different from those in Mina. In Mina the tents are made of heavy-duty canvas and are huge and fully equipped. These tents are smaller, colourful, with a red and blue pattern on the inside and a white and green stripe on the outside, and more what I had in mind when I had imagined it all in my head. There is no airconditioning, but more flaps have been left open, and it is actually better and healthier with the breeze wafting through.

We can rest now, the Imam tells us. *Wuqoof* will start after the midday prayers. We are not to engage in idle chatter with one another, but to spend this very valuable time in remembrance of God.

My blanket is thick and soft, and is folded in four, giving me the greatest cushioning effect for my back. But I cannot fall sleep immediately. I am in a tent with 160 people. If I move my foot two inches to the left or right, I am touching my neighbour's head. I am hearing snoring and sighs of fatigue. And too much has happened for me to doze off without replaying the day's events in my mind. Yesterday's long walk to Mina is already a thing of the distant past. I am lying thinking, Why we are doing all this, within these stipulated times? It's because our beloved Prophet Muhammad (pbuh) did the very same before us.

The holy Prophet (pbuh) had spent nine years in Medina without offering the pilgrimage. In his tenth year it was announced to all people that he would be performing hajj. People flocked to Medina to follow his guidance.

The following is a translation of the detailed report of the Prophet's pilgrimage (pbuh) given by Jabir ibn Abdullah, one of his young companions who reported a large number of *hadiths* (sayings and teachings of the Prophet, pbuh). This report forms the basis of many of the rulings and opinions given by the different schools of thought with regard to the pilgrimage and its duties and practices.

'When we arrived at the House (the Kab'ah in Mecca) with the Prophet (pbuh), he touched the corner (the Black Stone), then moved in a jogging movement for three rounds (circuits), and walked the

other three. He then went to Maqam Ibraheem and recited: "Make the place where Abraham stood as a place of prayer."

'He performed two *rak'ahs*, and recited Al-Ikhlas and Al-Kaffiroon. He then returned to the Black Stone and kissed it, after which he left through the door nearer to the hill of Al-Safa. The holy Prophet (pbuh) performed the *saee* between the hills of Safa and Marwah.

'When he reached Al-Safa, he read: "Safa and Marwah are among the symbols set up by God. Whoever visits the Sacred House for pilgrimage or *umrah* would do no wrong to walk to and fro between them. He who does good of his own accord shall find that God is most Thankful, All Knowing (2:158)."

'On the Day of Tarwiyah (8 Dhul-Hijjah) they proceeded to Mina resolving to do the pilgrimage. The Prophet (pbuh) mounted his camel and prayed at Mina the prayers of Zuhr, Asr, Maghrib, Isha and Fajr (meaning that he stayed all day and throughout the night).'

All these rituals leading up to and following the Prophet's (pbuh) stay in Mina constitute what Muslims have to do in order to perform hajj.

9.00 a.m. I am woken up by the buzz in the tent. They are serving koeksisters for breakfast. I have nothing except water to go with them, and cannot buy the tea they sell outside as it has caffeine. I have mango juice and a bottle of water. Afterwards, I go out to the ablution facilities. The toilets here are even more primitive. But I manage. By this stage, I have become an expert. However, I still have flu.

Back in the tent, the mood is sombre. People are reading from their Qur'ans or *kitaabs*. Some are reciting, some doing *thik'r*. There is no idle talk. We are served an excellent mutton breyani for lunch. We perform the midday prayers. Not long after, we are summoned to go outside the tent, where we will perform *wuqoof*.

We are a great number of people in front of the tent. We had brought white umbrellas for the sun, but the sky is strangely overcast. The Imam starts to recite the *duah* for *wuqoof*. We are to repeat after him in Arabic. It is long and goes on for more than an hour. Another man takes over, and then another, and another, then back to Imam Abdullah for the closing. Voices are breaking. The men are emotional. One of them cries as he talks to God: 'If you don't forgive us, God, who will?'

We are finished, and hug one another, and say, '*Haj Maqbool*. May Allah accept all your *dua'hs*, *Inscha Allah*.' We still have to go to Muzdalifah and pelt, and spend two more days at Mina and pelt again, but we have performed *wuqoof*. Our sins have been forgiven. If there is any doubt in our minds about that, our hajj has lost its validity. We are now hajjis.

There is no time to celebrate. We have to pack up again, and get ready to move. We have even more luggage because of the blankets. But we are not going to leave the blankets behind as they have made a difference to our backs at night, and we still have two more days at Mina after Muzdalifah, as well as a trip back to Mecca and back to Mina again.

4.00 p.m. We get on the bus. I don't know it yet, of course, but this will turn out to be the most nightmarish part of the whole hajj. Three million people are at Mina. They all have to leave for Muzdalifah to pick up the 49 stones to pelt the Jamarahs, and will stay until after midnight before proceeding to Mina, where they will pelt again.

We get into the bus with our bags and blankets and bottles of water. All around us people are standing waiting in groups. Buses are lined up, filled to overflowing, with many sitting on the roofs. Our bus moves forward two feet, and stops. The hooting is incessant as the drivers become agitated and hoot at one another back and forth, demanding space to move. We get into the bus at 4.00 p.m., and by 6.00 p.m., we have moved 50 metres. We are watching the day change into night.

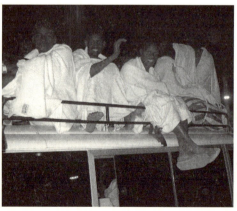

Driving a bus during hajj under these conditions requires guts, ability and the taking of special precautions. Next to the driver sits his assistant, who leans out of the bus and tells him to move more this way or that way, shouts at other bus drivers to get out of the way, and runs in between the buses to see what's going on or to have a chat. The process is agonisingly slow. I notice two assistants from other buses going out to buy coffee, which they enjoy with a cigarette, leaning against the back of a truck. I also notice a black woman getting out of a bus, lifting up her dress and squatting right between the narrow space between two buses. She gets up, rearranges her dress, and gets back on the bus. Not a minute later, a man gets off the same bus, squats between the two buses, and also leaves a big dark pool. What can you do? You've been in the bus for two hours already, and you haven't moved.

There are 68 people in our bus, with several men sitting on the roof. People are jammed up in the aisle. Even some women are left standing. One of the men on the roof gets off to go to the toilet, when suddenly the bus jerks into action and we're off. The bottleneck has cleared – there's an opening. Everyone races to get through. There's loud shouting as the man who got off the roof tries to catch up with the bus. He makes it, the door swings open, and he's on.

Then the fighting between the bus driver and his assistant begins. The driver is a slight, nimble and feisty Egyptian who, despite the overcrowded conditions in the bus and the fact that the airconditioning is not working, lights up a cigarette and smokes while he drives. It isn't easy driving in Mecca. A Cape Town driver would never make it. The drivers are jockeys, taking chances, cutting in front of other drivers, hooting and shouting.

We are on the road now, with buses on all sides of us. The pattern is the same for all the buses. A bus races ahead, sits on the tail of the bus in front, and then brakes suddenly. This happens over and over again. Our nerves are shot as the driver goes on and off the shoulder of the road, whipping up dust. The assistant shouts at him. He shouts back. The assistant stands over him and shouts louder. The driver takes his eyes off the road to fight back. I know from the girl sitting next to me, who lives in Bahrain and speaks Arabic, that the assistant is telling the driver that he can't drive, and that the driver is saying he has driven millions of people in Egypt. The assistant shouts that he is not in Egypt now. They almost come to blows.

The people in the bus are upset. We are in the hands of two madmen. Then suddenly the bus behind us shoots by us on the left and goes off the shoulder, down the hill. We are shouting now as we watch the bus veer to its left with all the people on the roof trying to clamber down. Any second now, the bus will topple over. The Imam shouts, '*Batcha* hard!' Pray hard! By some unbelievable miracle, the driver of the bus manages to get the bus back up the hill, and onto the road.

Meanwhile, the dust in our bus is overpowering and we are choking on the petrol fumes. Many of us are wearing facemasks. For the rest of the way, I am clutching my overnight bag on my lap, expecting at any time that someone will collide with us. Then there's a commotion at the back of the bus and we hear a loud crash. It has happened. A yellow bus passes us on the right with two of its windows broken. There's no insurance. You don't stop for details. You drive on. You have to be at all these places at very specific times of the day.

The Imam's voice rises up over the din. We will stop in Muzdalifah for only one hour to pray, and then move on to Mina, where we will pelt Aqaba. We cannot leave Muzdalifah until after a few minutes past midnight. We continue. We had got onto the bus at 4.00 p.m; finally, after a dizzying and frightening drive on the highway, we arrive in Muzdalifah at 11.30 p.m. A twenty-minute ride has taken almost seven and a half hours! The Imam tells us just to pick up our pebbles, and then perform *salaah*. But some of us have to go to the toilet. We have been sitting in the bus for many hours. We have stopped along the side of the road just as you come into Muzdalifah, away from the crowds. The Imam tells us to go up into the mountain. We are happy to do so: we have our water bottles, and can perform ablution afterwards. We

are about to walk up when the announcement is made again that we will drive on further and go to the public toilets.

A big mistake! We get back onto the bus, and because the road is so full of vehicles, a bus can only stop where it finds an opening along the side of the road. The moment we stop, however, another bus is behind us, and then another and another, and we're hemmed in. This means that we cannot leave for Mina until all the buses begin moving off, which will be at dawn. This is not at all what we had wanted to do. We had wanted to go to Mina as soon as possible, pelt the Jamarah, and then walk to Mecca, where we would only have had to leave our things at the hotel, perform ablution and go to the Haram to perform our *iefalda tawaaf* and *saee*. Being hemmed in by the other buses would set us back by several hours, because after the *iefalda tawaaf* and *saee*, we still had to return to Mina before the sunset prayers for two more days. If we waited until dawn to leave for Mina, we would have no time to rest in the hotel before leaving again.

Day 38 – Thursday January 20th 2005

It's thirty minutes past the midnight hour. Twenty of us decide not to stay with the bus, but to walk to Mina to pelt, and then head for Mecca. We take our bags off the bus – I'm carrying a blanket too now – and start walking. It's a brisk walk in the middle of the night, but we're in the company of thousands of pilgrims. There's no stopping now. We push on. Some of the people who have come with us are now way behind. Someone asks the man holding the South African flag if he can walk a bit more slowly and wait for the others. He says, No, he's not waiting: those who can't keep up must find their own way. There is a sense of urgency. We have been on the go non-stop. The patience one felt the day before has dissipated. It's everyone for themselves. You can't afford to wait.

We reach Mina about four hours later. But it is still too early to pelt. We have to wait for the *athan* to sound and perform *faj'r* prayers before we can do this. We approach the wide bridge where the Jamarah is and start walking up. At around 5.40 a.m. we hear the call to prayer and throw down our mats. There are thousands of people on the bridge already, all waiting to pray, and thousands more approaching. There are only seven of us. We have a quick discussion. We will pray, not make any long *duahs*, and as soon as the prayers are over, pick up our mats and start moving towards the Jamarah. We are to stick close together, hold on to one another, and not get lost. We are to pelt and to keep moving. In the event that we do get lost, we are to meet under the big neon sign at the bottom of the bridge.

But we are fortunate. Because we have walked, we have hundreds of thousands of pilgrims behind us, and we get to the Jamarah without too much shoving. We pelt our seven stones at the concrete pillar, saying *Bismillahi Allahu Akbar!* with every throw. It is the devil we're pelting. With every throw we are willing it to stay away. We are rejecting evil. We don't want it in our lives.

We wrestle our way out of the crowd and find each other. We are dead tired. To take the straight road to Mecca through the pedestrian tunnel means that we will not come across any kind of transportation, and will have to walk for several hours more. We take a left turn into the city, and walk along the main road. 'Haram,' we say to one taxi driver after another. The taxis are all occupied already. We drag ourselves along with our bags. After some time we find one driver who is willing to take us to the Haram, but two other people jump in first, and only four out of our group can squeeze into the car. I am left behind, although my luggage is in the boot. Together with the other two men, I walk on. Finally, we find a man with a bakkie who tells us to jump on the back; I have to climb up to get in. Another man – an assistant again – stands in the corner of the bakkie and somehow manages to convey to the driver via the mirror which way to go. We sail down into the city, the wind whipping at our clothes. We are dropped off near the Haram, and walk another ten minutes before we reach the hotel.

There is no time to waste. The Haram will be teeming with pilgrims, and we still have to do the *iefalda tawaaf* and *saee*. This is what everyone has been warning us about: not to get caught up in this *tawaaf* when it is at its busiest. My roommates and I take a quick *wudu* and walk up to the Haram for the 5.34 a.m. prayers. Where we decide to thrown down our mats is not too full yet. After prayers, we walk to the first level to perform the *tawaaf*. I have dreaded the complications inherent in the shoving and pushing of this *tawaaf*, but I see that despite the size of the crowd already there, it is manageable, and I decide to do it on my own. I had walked from Muzdalifah to Mina after midnight and I had walked halfway into Mecca. And now I was going to do seven circuits around the Kab'ah, which would take an hour, and then seven bouts of walking to and fro between Safa and Marwah to do the *saee*, taking another hour or more.

It's a huge moment for me, to find myself doing this on my own. I had been afraid of crowds. I had worried over the crushing hordes of people who would all descend on the Haram to come to do their *iefalda tawaaf*. And I didn't want anyone around me. I wanted to be by myself.

My body is weary, my throat is constricted with flu, but I can't afford to think. I can't be dwelling on my fatigue now. I have to keep moving. My feet are working independently of my mind and I am carried along with the stream. One circuit. Two circuits. Three circuits. Round and round, talking to God, until I have talked myself out, and completed all seven circuits.

At seven o'clock I am finished with the *tawaaf*. I had agreed to meet my roommates under the green light where the *tawaaf* begins and ends, so that we could all perform the *saee* together. I wait. No one pitches. It's Eid. The Eid prayers are about to begin. I walk away slowly to the section in the Haram where pilgrims are performing the *saee*. This area is even more congested than where I have just come from. I say *bismillah*, and step into the crowd.

As I walk I become aware of a dull ache in my back. I have been walking since midnight. I have special supportive soles that I wear in my Nikes, but for the *tawaaf* and the *saee*, you have to be either barefooted or in socks, unless you wear *qoophs* – soft black leather socks which protect your feet, but give no support. I had inserted these inner soles into my *qoophs* and had performed all seven circuits of the *tawaaf* in them, but I am now about to embark on the *saee* and my feet are sore. When I move my torso even a little to the left, I feel as if there's a knife lodged between my ribs. I can't walk any more. I have been on the move without a break. But I do it – up the corridor to one hillock, and then down the other – seven times. An hour later, I have finished. I cannot believe it. I have done this most important *tawaaf* and *saee*, and have done them on my own. I change into my walking shoes, and head for the hotel. I am tired. My eyes want to close. But I have a shower first and then drop into bed. When I awake, it is two hours past the midday prayers.

3.00 p.m. We are back downstairs in the hotel lobby because 160 of us have to get a bus to go back to Mina. Once more we are packed, although we carry a lighter load now. I have left behind the biscuits and the almonds and the umbrella and the torch. Still, I have my overnight bag, my folded blanket and my prayer mat. We are told to go up the road, where we will find the bus. This is not a bus contracted to

the group, but one that is there for anyone who wants to go to Mina, and all of Mecca is going to Mina. It is a nightmare. We have to go back to Mina to stay two more nights and do two more peltings of all three Jamarahs, but as I look at the eager crowd milling about in thick groups, all waiting for a bus to arrive, I wonder how we are going to get on.

The Imam hands out our tickets so that we may give them individually to the driver. He tells us that when the bus arrives, the men must 'block' the bus, and try to be first to get to the doors to let the group on. But what follows is something out of a horror movie. The bus arrives and immediately 50 or more people are hanging onto its sides, onto the doors, banging, shouting, but the driver refuses to stop and keeps edging forward until the bus is almost where we are all standing.

The push towards the door and the rush to get on are so severe that three or more people are jammed together at the entrance, and no one can lift a leg to get on. There is shouting, screaming. Someone is yelling, 'Help the Imam!' A woman with a child is almost crying. I am about six or more people behind, worrying what I will do if the bus is full and I don't manage to get on. I can't go on a different bus by myself. And so out of panic and fear, I also push to get to the door. The person in front of me is on the step of the bus. There is no more room. But I shout for him to move forward, and manage to get my foot on the step next to his. The driver, who doesn't speak a word of English, is trying to see out the side-view mirror of the bus, and yells for us to move out of the way. I don't budge. If I get off the bus now, I know I won't have the courage to go by myself to Mina in a different bus. And so the door of the bus slides closed just behind me, and I'm on.

The bus is so full that no one knows who's on the bus because the aisle is packed with people sitting on top of one another. Because I'm virtually on the step and blocking the side-view mirror, someone suggests that I sit on the floor. I do that but I can't breathe there, and what little air there is reeks with fumes from the constant moving and stopping of the bus, and from all the other vehicles and buses on the road. My throat is dry from dust particles and stale air. I am hot and uncomfortable, I have bad flu and I wonder how the holy Prophet (pbuh) made this journey fourteen hundred years ago on camels with hundreds of thousands of followers. A bus ride which ordinarily should take about 30 minutes or less takes three hours. But we are still lucky. I am told later by the sheikh's wife, who was in a different bus, that their bus had a puncture: the driver didn't only fix it himself, he went back into Mecca with all of them on board to deliver the tyre, and only then took them to Mina. They sat in the bus for five and a half hours.

This is hajj: this is what all the lessons were about. There are three million *hujaj* counting the Saudis. What makes it difficult is that all of them have to perform the same rituals at the same time, at the same places. It takes an awful lot of planning and managing and traffic control to pull

off such a feat. And they do. It's a tribute to the Saudi government that there aren't more fatalities.

We arrive in Mina, an hour's walk from where the South African camp is. The Imam discovers that a certain couple aren't on the bus, and they decide to wait for the next bus before going to the campsite. It is dark and I'm too tired to hang about, so I decide to walk on with a young couple who also don't want to wait. It is easier to walk in a small group if you have to walk through the crush of people, and I know the road through the tunnel will be full. Because we are only three, we can dodge through the crowd and get to the camp in 40 minutes. By the time the others arrive, we have already settled ourselves down in the tent and had an hour's rest. I am hungry, but am told that there will be no food served that night. I have dates and fruit in my bag, but am not in the mood for them. Another woman across the way from me says she has some crackers and a tin of tuna. We share it, and I throw myself down for the night. I am aware of the *thik'r* in progress in the men's tent, but am too fatigued to chant along for more than a few seconds. The world closes happily about my head.

Day 39 – Friday January 21st 2005

4.00 a.m. I am woken up, and come out of a deep sleep. Seven of us are not going to wait for the group and are going right away to pelt the Jamarahs. I manage a quick toilette, perform ablution, drink a glass of water, and am ready with my shoes on, carrying my mat.

It is a 45-minute walk back down the way we've come, but we take a different, back route to the Jamarah. The streets are packed with pilgrims: those heading to where we are, and those parked along the side of the street on blankets, sheets of cardboard and mattresses, or in tents – people lying on their sides, sprawled out, curled up, huddled together, sitting in groups eating, praying, reciting. We hold onto one another. We walk single file through the crowd. We step over people, into litter, into puddles, onto soggy plastic bags. We walk through the

bodies, around them, between them. We want to be on the bridge to pelt the first Jamarah by *faj'r* at 5.36 a.m. But there are thousands of other pilgrims also heading the same way, who have all had the same idea.

We reach the foot of the bridge. It is swarming with bodies, but the flow looks good. We wait for the call to prayer. A few minutes later, we hear it and throw down our mats and perform *salaah*. When we are done, we move immediately and take our little cloth bags with the 21 stones, and count out seven pebbles with which to pelt the first Jamarah. We brace ourselves and start walking. We will aim our pebbles at the stone pillar, say *Bismillahi Allahu Akbar*, and then pelt again until we have thrown all seven stones. Again, we are fortunate. Because of the early hour, and because a large majority of pilgrims will pelt only after midday, the *zahmah* is manageable, and there's no shoving and pushing. We are easily able to extricate ourselves and move on to the next Jamarah a few hundred feet away. Last year 250 pilgrims died in the crush. Since then, the Saudi government has built a bridge over the Jamarah and you can pelt both upstairs and downstairs. Also, the stone pillar has been made wider, which means people don't have to crush together to be able to hit it. In addition, once you have pelted, you now move to the exit, whereas before people pelted and came back out the same way as they had entered, causing congestion.

Unfortunately, two people from India have died while pelting the Jamarah this year – both from cardiac arrest.

We arrive at the next Jamarah, and the next. At last we are finished. We have to come back tomorrow morning for a last pelting, and then our hajj rituals will be complete and we can go back to Mecca. We move with the crowd and take a right turn down the bridge to go back to the camp. The walk back is slower because of the thousands of pilgrims heading for the bridge, and we arrive in a little under an hour. The rest of our group is still in the tent. They are going only after the midday prayers. I am grateful that we are done. At midday the bridge is going to be teeming with pilgrims, and with the hot sun beating down on their heads, it will not be easy.

I am back in the tent now, making notes. I have to make notes whenever I can, and as soon as I conveniently can, because the days tend to blend into one another, and one can forget or become con-

fused. Half the women are still asleep, others are up. We are in the same clothes that we arrived in. There's no luxury of changing into pyjamas. You have to be in and out of the tent, going to the toilet or taking ablution, and mingling with the opposite sex. You have to be dressed at all times to be ready to pray, or to leave.

I am watching a particular woman now who is sitting in a corner with her back to the group. She is peering into a small mirror, applying mascara to lashes already thickened with make-up. I am amazed. This is a spiritual camp-out. I had already noticed her heavy eye make-up – drawn to perfection like Cleopatra's – at the beginning of the trip. Not a lash out of place, and make-up perfectly applied. And she's not a young woman. I am wondering how that eyebrow pencil and mascara don't smudge with all the ablution we have to take. The rest of us look scrubbed clean and basic. In a way, though, I admire her also. It's the little things that keep you sane.

11.00 a.m. Sheikh Gabriels' wife and I have a good hour of interesting conversation. I see that we have much in common. We are both interested in the past, in the prophets, in the reading and translation of the Qur'an. In addition to a great many subjects we talk about, she has an interesting take on how to have a successful 'squat'. Something about the left knee being tucked up under the stomach (she shows me), and the right knee being freer. According to her, this position allows the larrge intestine to do its job properly.

'If you squat like this,' she says, 'it will all happen miraculously.'

I laugh, but am not rushing out to try it. I will wait for the civilised facilities of the hotel.

12.00 p.m. The rest of the group leave to go to pelt. It is scorching hot outside the tent. Men are told to wear scarves on their heads. They have been given three options: (1) to pelt now, at the recommended time, after *zawahl*; (2) to pelt tomorrow morning after *faj'r*, come down the bridge, and do it a second time; or (3) to go to pelt on their own, or have it done by proxy, i.e. if someone is weak or ill or unable to pelt, someone else can do it for them. That person first pelts for himself, then does it for the other person. I am enormously grateful that we have already done our first pelting at dawn that morning.

It will be our last day and night in the tent. We're exhausted. We're served an excellent mutton curry for lunch. The group comes back from pelting. They had gone with pilgrims from three other South African groups, about 200 in number, and had arrived at the bridge to a heavy *zahmah*. The men had formed a chain around the women, and in this fashion they approached the Jamarah – effectively blocking outsiders from penetrating and breaking up the group. They were able to pelt without incident, and come back safely.

8.00 p.m. My last night in the tent. I am filled with strange emotions. I have forged new friendships, and have been together with these women – young and old – for a concentrated period of time. I am discovering them in a way I haven't before – without their men – and am gaining some wonderful insights. It's an enjoyable passage of time. We are here for hajj, but it's not all spirituality and *ibadah*. There's laughter and a few quiet jokes, and I will take home with me a few choice expressions.

Our last pelting of the three Jamarahs will take place tomorrow at dawn, after which we will have successfully completed our hajj. I can't believe that I have done all this. That I have managed to perform all the rituals and that I have survived. More than anything, I feel a great cleansing, and a sense that I've achieved something. For the first time now, after everything I've been through, I feel worthy of having been forgiven. I have earned this forgiveness: not with my pocket book or my time, but with my heart and my sincerity to please God. My slate has been wiped clean. The hardest part will be to keep it from being messed up again. I will have to try hard. I don't know if a second invitation will come; and your first hajj is your most significant.

After tomorrow morning's pelting, we will go back to Mecca and rest up for a few days before returning to South Africa. Our last devotion will be the *wieda tawaaf*, where we will do a final seven circuits and bid farewell to the Kab'ah. After you have performed *wieda*, you cannot come back to do another *tawaaf*.

I am tearful as I write this. I am changed in some way. I can't describe how. I have become emotional very many times. I know that if I had lived in the Prophet's time (pbuh), I would've been a model citizen, but I'm not from that time. I will have to call on all my reserves when I get home.

While scribbling these notes down in my book, I am listening to the men in the next tent. I will miss the *thik'r*. I will miss Imam Abdullah's voice. The *thik'r* picks up in tempo, and I glance towards the slit in the tent. I can see the men swaying back and forth. The *thik'r* is altogether too hypnotic and riveting. I will miss it. I am not gone yet – and it has been the hardest thing I've done in my life – but I know I will be back again.

It is said that God comes down to the first *samaah* during hajj. I don't know if our brains can comprehend what this really means, but I know that in a very real way, I have moved closer to God. Hajj is a jihad – fraught with hardship and lessons along the way. I am grateful for the invitation extended to me, and even more grateful that hajj had been made obligatory for me. Had I not been ordered to do it, I would not have gone on my own and would not have had the experience. In Mecca I became aware of my mortality, and the fact that with every passing day I was one step closer to the next world. Muslims prepare for the next world. The degree of spirituality you have here is the level of spirituality you leave with. The idea is not to leave with a thin packet. More than this awareness, though, is discovering your own shortcomings. In Mecca I sat still long enough to take stock. I couldn't escape the reality of the things I lacked in my life – and the areas that could do with improvement.

Day 40 – Saturday January 22nd 2005

I am woken up shortly after 4.00 a.m. to go pelting. My bag is packed already. I will leave behind the blanket. After the pelting, we will head straight for Mecca.

After a date and a glass of water, we're off. We reach the bridge almost an hour before the *faj'r* prayers. We wait, and watch more and more pilgrims arrive. By the time the *athan* sounds, the bridge is packed with bodies. All are ready to pray and head directly for the Jamarah. We do the same. Again, because we are there at this hour, we are able to manoeuvre ourselves through the crowd and get close enough to the stone pillar to pelt. Fifteen minutes later, we have pelted all three Jamarahs, and are on our way. There is a streak of lightning across the sky. I look up. Another bolt lights up the sky. Mecca has been praying for rain. It has rained four or five times a year. Wouldn't this be appropriate, I thought, if after the completion of hajj, we would get rain now? Would this be God's blessing?

We start to walk. We feel the first drops. It will take us two or more hours to walk to Mecca unless we get a taxi. Ahead of us are thousands of pilgrims, and behind. We pick up pace and head for the main road. The traffic is so congested that it doesn't pay to think of asking anyone for a ride. After half an hour of walking, I see an Arab leaning against a van. I say to him, 'Haram?' He nods. 'How many rials?' I ask. He holds up two fingers. 'Okay,' we agree. For the seven of us, it will be twenty rials each, which makes 140 rials. I would've paid double that just to get into the taxi and be driven to the hotel. The rain is coming down hard now as we reach the vicinity of the Haram. You never get driven to the doorway. One of the men pays the driver with a 200 rial note. The driver doesn't have change, but he sees another taxi next to his, and right in the middle of the main road, with cars behind him, he stops and gets out and asks the taxi driver for change. He receives the change and gets back into the vehicle. The cars behind us hoot while he counts out the correct change. We get out and walk to the hotel in the rain. We have colds and sore throats, and get wet during the ten-minute walk, but we're too grateful to be back in Mecca. It is just after seven in the morning when we reach the hotel. We sleep until noon.

12.35 p.m. We go down to the hotel lobby for the midday prayers. I am shocked by what I see outside the door. People on their way to the Haram are soaking wet. Mecca is flooded with rain, with the water reaching up to their knees. People go upstairs for their cameras. After prayers, even the sheikh joins in and stands knee-deep in water, posing for a photograph. The next day in the papers it is reported that a whole family in a car died in the flood in Medina, while two people died in Mecca. The rain, which had been prayed for, hadn't come like this in twenty years.

Day 41 – Sunday January 23rd 2005

I sleep until ten, then get down to typing up my notes for the past five days. There will be no time when I get home. And this is the kind of thing that has to get written right away.

Day 42 – Monday January 24th 2005

My sore throat is back, but I refuse to take more antibiotics. After lunch we are told that our Cairo to Johannesburg flight on the 28th has been delayed by seven hours, and that we will have to stay one night in Cairo. Also, that we will miss our connecting flight from Johannesburg to Cape Town, and will have to stay overnight there also, and arrive a day late.

Day 43 – Tuesday January 25th 2005

Sick in bed.

Day 44 – Wednesday January 26th 2005

Wake up in a sweat for *faj'r* prayers. Barely able to get out of bed and perform ablution. Feel dizzy in the toilet while brushing my teeth, and have to sit down for a few minutes before continuing. I pray and go back to bed and sleep until 9.00 a.m. It's my intention to walk to the hospital, but I'm afraid to go alone. Also, I don't want any more antibiotics. I decide that the worst is over, and that I will have to ride it out. With a lot of encouragement from my roommates, I go with two of them to the Hilton to buy an ice cream, which helps a lot.

Feeling better in the afternoon. Tomorrow I will have to be strong to perform my final *tawaaf*.

Day 45 – Thursday January 27th 2005

Wake up feeling much better. Go for a walk in the morning to see how I hold up, and decide to do the final *wieda tawaaf* with the people I came with. However, they decide to perform the *wieda tawaaf* at midnight, come back at two in the morning, skip sleep, and then wait for the bus, which will pick us up at eight in the morning. Our luggage has to be in the foyer by 6.30 a.m. I'm not one of those people who can miss a night's sleep, especially when sick, then sit for twelve hours at Jeddah airport to wait for a flight. I go for a solo final *tawaaf* at nine and find that the Haram is full. I haven't had a *tawaaf* in several days owing to my sore throat and cold. Once again I cannot believe, when I look at the Kab'ah, that I am here. My whole life I have faced in the direction of the Kab'ah to pray, and here I am in front of it. And I know that once I am done, I cannot come back, and that I must not waste time leaving Mecca after making my final *tawaaf*.

I am not as strong as I'd like to be, and the first two circuits take particularly long. And then I get my second wind, and get into the rhythm. I have my dialogue with God. I have always had my dialogues with God at home, but in Mecca they have been different for me. I am not so naïve as to believe that God was not at home with me, and that He is in Mecca, for God says in the Qur'an that He is closer to you than your jugular vein. Still, I feel a very strong presence of God. I feel touched. I feel listened to. I feel good.

When the seven circuits are over, I pray on my mat and thank God for having inspired me to come and for having allowed me to perform my *umrah* and hajj and complete all my rituals. I ask Him to allow me to return home safely to my family – and to allow me to come back again. I fold up my prayer mat, stand at the railing for a while to look at the Kab'ah, then bid it farewell, and turn my back to it to go. I am sad. I will leave at eight in the morning: I won't see the Kab'ah again. I will miss the routine and will dearly miss the voice of the imam in the Haram. I am misty-eyed as I walk back. Even though it is after ten, the streets are brimming with life and vitality. Mecca never sleeps. It's a constantly changing wheel of human beings.

Day 46 – Friday January 28th 2005

We are up at 4.30 a.m., and down in the lobby with all our bags and cases by 6.30. The bus arrives at 8.30. It takes an hour to load the bags

onto the roof. We pick up four other South African pilgrims at a different hotel and it is after eleven before we are on our way. We go first to where departing pilgrims have to check in. We remain on the bus; the driver, a Nigerian, has a manifest of all the pilgrims on the bus, as well as a bag full of pass-

ports and airline tickets. We were not in possession of our passports while in Mecca. Names are checked against the list, and after some time, we depart.

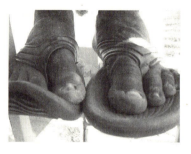

Halfway to Jeddah on the highway, someone shouts that one of the bags, secured by ropes, is threatening to fall off the bus. The driver stops. The ladder comes out. He gets on top of the bus, where the canvas covering all the bags has also come undone. Three others help him reinforce the ropes and we drive on. The bag comes down again, but doesn't fall off. Passing cars hoot at us. Again we stop in the middle of the expressway. We stop three times before we reach the Hajj Terminal: we are back at Tent City. It is now just after 1.00 p.m. and we have to pray. The terminal is alive and teeming with pilgrims – all laden with bags – many of them camped out on flattened cardboard and mats.

Our luggage is put on two big carriers, and we follow it to a spot where there is enough room for our group to sit and wait. The bags are positioned in a circle. In the middle of the circle, we throw down our prayer mats. We will be in the airport until 10 p.m., so we have nine hours to go. All around us are weary-eyed pilgrims. Some have been there since dawn, others for more than 24 hours. Their blankets and goods are all over the plastic benches and the floor. Their flights have been delayed several times. They don't believe they will ever get out of the air-

port. There are no announcements. No postings of flights. The man in charge of our group, Sabri, has all our passports and tickets, and goes off to get our boarding passes. Boarding passes are provided for the group, not individually. He comes back after an hour and says there's no plane.

'What do you mean there's no plane?' someone asks.

'There's no plane,' he says. 'We're not even leaving at ten o'clock.'

I look around. I had prepared myself for the worst. I had heard about pilgrims spending whole days and nights at Jeddah's Hajj

Terminal. It's nothing new: hundreds of thousands of passengers have to leave. Only one plane can take off at a time. A confirmed flight doesn't mean a thing – we all have confirmed flights. But we're not leaving any time soon, and there's no indication when we might.

We buy tea and chicken and rice. The next *waq't* arrives. We sit on our prayer mats on the ground, some of us with our heads on our overnight bags, trying to have a nap.

At ten o'clock that night we still don't know when we're leaving. Sabri has been to the office several more times, each time coming back with no news. We have a connecting flight in Cairo at ten in the morning. We console ourselves that as long as we are there by that time, we won't panic. We are told further that if we miss that flight, Cairo only has two flights a week to Johannesburg, on Tuesdays and Thursdays.

The night passes with Sabri going every hour or so to check if we are any closer to getting a flight. Finally, he comes back and says we are leaving at 2.00 a.m. But he will have to go back for our boarding passes. An hour later we are told that the plane has been given to another group: we have to wait.

At 4.00 in the morning, when we are half-asleep on cardboard and benches, we are told to hurry up – we have to go to the gate. We arrive there and stand in line for an hour. Finally, an official comes forward and holds up a blue boarding pass and says that everyone with a boarding pass of that colour can come through. There is panic and pandemonium as travellers try to barge through the narrow gate. I have my overnight bag, my laptop, a bag of dates and a trolley, but the entrance is so narrow that I can't get through, and have to leave my 35 rial trolley behind. After moving from one room to another – sitting, waiting, watching other passengers who are booked onto the flight before ours getting into a verbal contest with an airport official – with the official making his own voice heard above everyone else's – we are finally told it is time to board at 6.00 a.m. A free Qur'an is handed to us before we board the plane. We are all asleep in our seats by the time it takes off.

Day 47 – Saturday January 29th 2005

We arrive in Cairo at 9.15 a.m. and are told to hurry to the gate as the plane for Johannesburg is taking off on time at ten. We are grateful – finally, a plane that will leave on time. Finally, some sanity. We rush to the gate. The security officers tell us there is no plane. They don't know when there'll be a plane for Johannesburg, and no reasons are given for the delay. We go to information. They tell us security don't know what they're talking about: the plane is there, and will leave on time. We go back. At ten we are still standing in line. There are no answers; no one knows anything. And this is Cairo International.

I go to ask whether we can check in and at least sit in the lounge. They give me a long story, a lot of which doesn't make sense to my South African brain. I make a fuss. Finally, we are allowed to check in. We swarm in like locusts and minutes later, there are no empty seats. For our inconvenience, we are given rolls and Pepsi. We sit, cramped and crumpled, between cases and boxes, too afraid to leave for fear that our places will be taken. But we have endured, and we will endure for a few hours longer.

Shortly before two, a bus pulls up, and we are told that we are leaving. We board the plane. Our scarves sit crooked on our heads, and we look a little bit the worse for wear, still in the same clothes in which we left Mecca at 6.30 a.m. on Friday morning – but we are going home. I am longing to be with my family, but as each mile brings me closer, I feel the energy of Mecca slipping slowly away. As the plane touches down on the runway in Johannesburg, I breathe a sigh of relief, but also feel a kind of despair. I am back in Sodom and Gomorrah. I am back in the belly of the beast, where it is that much harder to be good.

It is evening. We have all missed our connecting flights. We are tired and have to get our luggage, go through Customs, and check in at the hotel that has been arranged for us. An hour after arrival we are still lined up with our trolleys reaching down the street. It takes two and a half hours before we get onto a shuttle and reach the hotel. I am thankful for the quiet elegance of the large room and also for the hot shower; and enormously grateful that I need share with only one person. It is my first real moment of privacy in almost seven weeks.

Day 48 – Sunday January 30th 2005

5.30 a.m. I wake up, take a shower and get dressed. Our plane to Cape Town leaves at a quarter to eleven, but we are not going to wait about for the others. If it took all those hours to move the pilgrims by shuttle to the hotel, it is going to take just as long to get them back to the airport. We want to be out first. By seven we are down in the lobby with our bags: we won't have breakfast. Twenty minutes later we are at the airport. We check in and go for coffee. It is my first decaffeinated cappuccino in seven weeks. I close my eyes in appreciation as I take the first sip. I am home. Even though I still have one lap to go, I am in my own country. The rigours of my travels already seem far away.

1.48 p.m. I am picked up at Cape Town International Airport, and arrive home to family and friends, and to an imam who makes the final *duah* for me before I enter the house. My sister and sisters-in-law have been there since seven that morning, preparing lunch and everything else. For the next ten hours I am surrounded by family and friends who have all come to hear about my experience. This will go on for seven days. People are all anxious to know what my trip was like. How was Mecca, they ask? How was hajj? But how can I tell them about Mecca in a sentence? Where do I start? I'm still reeling from the experience, and it will take some time to put it all in perspective.

It is after midnight when the last visitor leaves. My suitcase is on the bedroom floor, open, with presents and clothes strewn on the bed. It is quiet. I can hear the gentle patter of the rain outside my window. I had promised God one thing when in Mecca: that I would never neglect my prayers again. And so there is one more thing for me to do before I can go to bed. I take ablution. I roll out my prayer mat. I perform my final *ishai* prayers.

Thank you, Allah. Thank you for having taken me safely to Mecca, and returning me safely again to my family. Thank you for looking after me, and thank you for the strength and the resolve to perform hajj. Thank you. Thank you.

Thursday March 17th 2005

Six weeks later. Editing *The Mecca Diaries*, and busy with auditions and rehearsals for the film of *Confessions of a Gambler*. My flu is gone. My life is hectic. But I've had time to look back and reflect. I miss Mecca, and wish sometimes that I could be back just for a few minutes, to savour again the peace that I'd felt. Hajj is a most gracious gift. It's an opportunity to review your life, a chance to become a better human being. How can I not be grateful for the chance to feel whole again?

10.30 p.m. The last of the cast members have gone. I am tired. My bed is waiting. But my promise: I have to keep it. Not for God, but for me.

Do's and Don'ts

- One of the most important things, when contemplating hajj and looking for a suitable package, is to think very carefully about your accommodation. Spend less on shopping and take that extra thousand to secure a room for two. You can go in a group of four or more, but only share with one person. It is too late when you get there to change things.

- If you are a non-smoker, do not travel with a smoker. Women aren't allowed to smoke in the street or in public places in Mecca and Medina, and will smoke in the room. This can create serious problems when you are allergic to smoke.

- Travel with someone you're very familiar with, i.e. mother and son, husband and wife, brother and sister. In other words, someone whose habits you know. This makes it easier to negotiate and establish the rules.

- Make sure that what is on your contract with the agent is what you get and, if it isn't what you find when you arrive at your hotel room, deal with it straight away. My cousin travelled with a different group. She and her brother and her brother's wife were to be in two rooms. When they arrived at the hotel, they were all put in the same room. The agent promised to do something about it. He never did. No money was refunded.

- Establish the rules at the beginning. Don't assume that people are like you. And don't be dogmatic in the way you put things across.

You might be an early riser, and go to bed early. Your roommate might want to go to bed only at three in the morning. Negotiate about things like lights and airconditioning.

- Put the airconditioning on when you leave to go out so that the room will be cool upon your return, and then switch it off.

- Don't pack unnecessary clothes when you leave. You need only two bras, two robes, two sets of *ihram*, three panties, two pairs of socks. You wash one and wear the other. Whatever you wash is dry within two hours.

- As well as all recommended vitamins and medications, bring along glycerine suppositories. For the days of Mina and Arafah, where you have substandard toilet conditions and stage fright, you don't want to prolong the discomfort.

- Take along a good pair of walking shoes so that if you decide to do the walking hajj, you are properly prepared. For the *tawaaf* and *saee*, buy a pair of *qoophs*. If you have special rubber inner soles for your shoes, put them in your *qoophs*. This will mean the difference between having back pain, or not.

- Have a good-sized cloth bag made, with a broad shoulder strap and a Velcro opening, that you can wear every day to the Haram. You can put your rolled up prayer mat in it, as well as your *qoophs*, your *kitaabs* and your tissues and glasses.

- Make sure that whatever antibiotics you take with you are clearly marked, and that you know what constitutes a full course. For instance, if you have a bladder infection, a full course might only be three days. If it's flu or bronchitis, it might be five. I can't stress enough how important this is. Don't stop taking your pills if you are feeling better after the first or second day, or you might end up taking antibiotics repeatedly.

- Bring along a piece of elastic to tie around your waist so that your robe and petticoat can be hoisted up around your hips when you go to the outside toilets.

- Bring along some pins and needle and thread.

- It is cool in the mornings in Medina. In addition to a jersey, take along a thin shawl. This can be used to cover your feet in the tent, or to drape over your shoulders in the bus.

- When leaving for Mina and Arafah, don't bother with the white umbrella or the torch. If you end up walking, it is all extra weight you have to carry. And you don't need two packets of biscuits or a kilo of dates, and all that water and juice: you can buy things along the way. However, a necessary item is the plastic bottle with the spray attachment. You can use this to take ablution in the tent, or if you have to go to the toilet and there is no water along the way.

- Don't take an overnight bag of the backpack type with cords: it will cut into your shoulders after a while because of the weight. Take wet wipes for your days in the tent. Also take a pair of flipflops that you can wear while standing in the shower, or when visiting the outside toilets, so that you can wash your feet – sandals and all – afterwards.

- Drink lots of *zamzam*, but balance it out with bottled water. And bottled *zamzam* is better than cooled *zamzam*, as the *zamzam* is chilled with ice blocks made from tap water.

- Have lots of patience and consideration for others.

Glossary

abayah cloak worn over clothes; a robe
aqaba great Satan pillar
asghari male or female security guard
asr mid-afternoon prayer time
athan the call to prayer
ayah verse from the Qur'an
bismillah 'in the name of God'
caliph Muslim teacher
duah individual prayer or supplication
dumm penaly for specific transgressions during haj
fajr dawn prayers, which must be performed between the first moment of dawn and sunrise
ghus'l total ritual ablution of the body; a separate wash after a shower
hadith a saying of the Holy Prophet (pbuh)
hajj annual pilgrimage to Mecca, centring on the five days spent between Mina, Arafah and Muzdalifah
haram holy or sacred precinct, more specifically the precincts including the Grand Mosque in Mecca or the Prophet's Mosque in Medina
hidaya inspiration from Allah
hujaj persons performing hajj
ibadah a duty towards Allah
iefalda tawaaf a compulsory circumambulation of the Kab'ah in Mecca as part of the hajj ritual
ihram clothing worn upon entering Mecca – white robes for women and two pieces of unstitched white towelling for men
ishai mid-evening prayers
istigarah special prayers seeking guidance from Allah
jamarah stone pillar or pillars at Mina which have to be pelted with stones during hajj
janazah funeral
jihad exertion in the path of God
jum'ah/jumah Friday prayers
kab'r grave or tomb

kitaab book containing religious writings
maghrib prayers performed after sunset
mahram person responsible for an unmarried woman during hajj
mataff marble precinct surrounding both the Grand Mosque in Mecca and the Prophet's Mosque in Medina where one can pray
miqat point from which a pilgrim can enter the holy city
muslah prayer mat
niyyah formal intention to do something
qibla the direction in which one faces during prayer
qoophs soft leather 'socks'
rak'ah set of prayers
sab'r to have patience
saee the act of walking to and fro seven times between the hills of Safa and Marwah
samaah the heavens
shuroots conditions, requirements
slavat money given as a gift
tanazul fee paid to Saudi Arabian authorities to cover airport taxes, etc
taqdir part of God's great plan
tawaaf circumambulation seven times around the Kab'ah
thuh'r midday prayer time
toekamandie a woman who washes and lays out the dead
umrah performing a *tawaaf* and a *saee* upon entering Mecca
waq't time for prayer
wieda tawaaf the final *tawaaf* at the end of hajj
wudu ablution
wuqoof prayers offered in Arafah from noon to the evening of the ninth day of the hajj
zahmah crowds present at religious gatherings
zamzam water from the sacred spring Zamzam in Mecca
zawahl noon
zuhr midday prayer-time